DANGEROUS FRIEND

DANGEROUS FRIEND

The Teacher-Student
Relationship
in
Vajrayana
Buddhism

RIG'DZIN DORJE

SHAMBHALA
Boston & London
2001

Shambhala Publications, Inc.
Horticultural Hall
300 Massachusetts Avenue
Boston, Massachusetts 02115
www.shambhala.com

9 8 7 6 5 4 3 2 1

First Edition
Printed in the United States of America

⊗ This edition is printed on acid-free paper that meets
the American National Standards Institute z39.48 Standard.
Distributed in the United States by Random House, Inc.,
and in Canada by Random House of Canada Ltd

Library of Congress Cataloging-in-Publication Data
Rig-'dzin-rdo-rje.
Dangerous friend: the teacher-student relationship in
Vajrayana Buddhism/ Rig'dzin Dorje.—Ist Shambhala ed.
p. cm.
Includes index.
ISBN 1-57062-857-2 (pbk.)
1. Spiritual life—Tantric Buddhism. 2. Teacher–student
relationships—Religious aspects—Tantric Buddhism.
3. Buddhism—China—Tibet—Doctrines. I. Title
BQ8939.5 .R55 2001
294.3'61—dc21

Dangerous Friend *is dedicated to the long life, good health, and unim-
peded activity of my root lamas, the Holders of Khyungchen Aro Lingma's
Aro gTér lineage: Ngak'chang Rinpoche, the incarnation of Aro Yeshé, and
Khandro Déchen, the incarnation of A-yé Khandro.*

*It is dedicated also to their root lamas: His Holiness Dud'jom Rinpoche,
His Holiness Dilgo Khyentsé Rinpoche, Kyabjé Künzang Dorje Rinpoche
& Jomo Sam'phel, gTértrül Chhi-'mèd Rig'dzin Rinpoche, and Khamtrül
Yeshé Dorje Rinpoche. Finally, although I have never had the great good
fortune to meet them, I especially dedicate this book to Dungsé Thrinlé
Norbu Rinpoche and Chögyam Trungpa Rinpoche.*

*May the authentic lineages of Vajrayana and their glorious lineage holders
prevail over the minions of spiritual materialism and the four philosophical
extremes for the benefit of everyone and everything everywhere.*

Amongst my greatest Lamas I include a butcher,
a prostitute, and a bandit.
Kyabjé Künzang Dorje Rinpoche

A paranoid dog's loud barking is disrespectful to thieves
but respectful to its master.
Dungsé Thrinlé Norbu Rinpoche, *Magic Dance*

The physician becomes wild, which is terrifying.
We do not want to trust a wild doctor or surgeon. But we must.
Chögyam Trungpa Rinpoche, *The Myth of Freedom*

The Lama is none other than your own vajra nature, so yes:
the ultimate vajra commitment is to your own vajra nature –
but only when you recognize that your mind is inseparable
from the mind of your vajra master.
Khandro Déchen, *Roaring Silence*

The Lama is the terrifyingly compassionate gamester
who reshuffles the deck of your carefully arranged rationale.
Ngak'chang Rinpoche, *Wearing the Body of Visions*

One thing to find a guide. Another to follow him.
Ted Hughes, "Badlands" from *The Birthday Letters*

Questions are never dangerous until you answer them.
John le Carré, *The Secret Pilgrim*

CONTENTS

ACKNOWLEDGMENTS

To acknowledge the influence of Ngak'chang Rinpoche and Khandro Déchen on this book would be so inadequate as to be ridiculous. This book was written at their urgent request, to help counterbalance the writings of those who misguidedly seek to modify the essential structure of the Vajrayana. My root lamas are deeply concerned with what they describe as "the perfidious publicity machine of a group of highly vocal western buddhist teachers, and their antagonism to authentic Vajrayana and its lineage lamas." They feel that, although vastly superior material on the role of the vajra master is available to the Buddhist public, much of this material could prove difficult reading for the majority of people most easily influenced by the smooth words of those who attempt to discredit the role of the vajra master. They also feel that a statement from a western disciple of western lamas would provide a cogent point of view; that is to say, I am not defending a culturally Tibetan position at the behest of a Tibetan lama. That I am a happily married man with a son and a family life serves to demonstrate the vivid appropriateness of the vajra master role to the west. Far from being an eastern mode that is inapplicable to western people, the traditional role of the vajra master is the very heart of all spiritual paths. The efforts of my root lamas to preserve the authentic Vajrayana in the west is expressed best by Dungsé Thrinlé Norbu

Rinpoche in his colophon to a long-life prayer he wrote for Kyabjé Künzang Dorje Rinpoche and Jomo Sam'phel, at the request of Ngak'chang Rinpoche and Khandro Déchen:

> Thus the world of the five great continents resounds. Residing in the western continent of Europe, an honorable holy hero, Ngak'chang Chö-ying Gyamtso Rinpoche, and his consort holy heroine, Khandro Déchen Tsédrüp Rolpa'i Yeshé, who have unshakable, reasonable faith in the general teachings of the Buddhas and especially the priceless teachings of the great Vajrayana and their lineage holders, are fearlessly shooting the cannonball of logic with great compassion in order to annihilate and put on the correct path of enlightenment all those wild beings who are misunderstanding, with a reverse point of view and with intent, the teachings of the Buddhas and lineage holders of the teachings of the Buddhas. From their request through the path of letters, I, Thinley Norbu, immediately wrote this in front of dakas and dakinis.

The forbearance of my lamas with the time it has taken me to write this book has been humbling. It has been a time within which their own fertile productivity has been astonishing by contrast. My dilatoriness must be added to the debt I owe them for the entire content and quality of the life I now lead. This is a debt which, in the nature of Vajrayana, cannot be less than total. It will always remain beyond the possibility of repayment. This is a typical Tantric paradox—a debt that buoys me up rather than weighing me down. Wherever I go to teach, I have the opportunity to repay the kindness and insight which my lamas have painstakingly invested in me for so long by being sure to bring Ngak'chang Rinpoche and Khandro Déchen to the awareness of others, as the constant focus of my gratitude. I wrote this book as a specific practice, as a servant of the Ngak'phang sangha of the Nyingma tradition. Any credibility it may possess derives from the authenticity of my root lamas, whilst its inadequacies represent the gulf between my ability and their example.

I have been inspired throughout by my ordained vajra sisters and brothers. That they are here in this world, dedicated to the *gö-ḳar-chang-lo* vows, and committed to practice with their vajra masters is a continuing inspiration. I remember the warmth and humanity of Ngakma Nor'dzin and Ngakpa 'ö-Dzin, the generosity and spiritual passion of Ngakma Yeshé, the dynamism and incisiveness of Naljorma Jig'mèd, the depth and spacious humour of Naljorpa Rang-rig, the enthusiasm and poise of Naljorma 'ö-Sel, and the kindness and stability of Naljorma Sel-zér Pamo. I think of them often, and when I do my heart lifts and I soar with confidence in the Buddhist refuge of Sangha and the future of the Vajrayana. Their love and unswerving devotion to Ngak'chang Rinpoche and Khandro Déchen is a shining example in a world where honor, integrity, and courage seem to have been forgotten. In a world in which we are taught to admire personal failure and the betrayal of promises on the basis of following transient feelings, my vajra sisters and brothers are a glorious example of the fact that it does not have to be that way. We can live with dignity, kindness, and honesty.

I am especially indebted to the subtle and pervasive intelligence, the comprehensively ironic wit, and the sensitive, trusting companionship of Ngakma Shardröl. As an editor she has the knack of mellowing discrimination with encouragement, and without her help this collection of words would never have become a book.

I would also like to thank my vajra brothers and sisters who helped with the research: Jaye Ann Ito (Dorje Khandro), David Chapman (A'gyür Rig-tsal), Naljorma Jig'mèd, Jill Grundberg (Pema Yeshé), Wendy Trefelner (Rig'dzin Lhamo), Ngakpa Namgyal, Ngakpa Seng-gé, and Wayne Grachow (Gyür'mèd Dorje).

Finally I owe thanks to my wife, Nicola, and my son, Henry (A-kyong Rig-tsal Tak-jung), for their love, patience, tolerance, and understanding.

FOREWORD

We enthusiastically and cheerfully acknowledge our glorious root lamas: Kyabjé Künzang Dorje Rinpoche and Jomo Sam'phel—incomparable personifications of compassion and wisdom; unexcelled vajra masters; and living embodiments of Padmasambhava and Yeshé Tsogyel. It is entirely to them that we owe the accomplishment of our disciple Rig'dzin Dorje.

Nga-la Rig'dzin Taklung Rolpa'i Dorje has written this most worthy text—sensitively edited by his vajra sister Ngakma Shardröl. *Dangerous Friend* is accessible, conversant with the times in which it will be read, and utterly sincere in what it communicates. It is a valuable reference work for anyone approaching the Vajrayana and making a serious commitment to a lama and a lineage. Rig'dzin Dorje's book is a timely testament to the importance of maintaining the authentic nature of Vajrayana in the face of widespread misunderstanding propagated by what we call the "conference Buddhism" of the 1990s. Unfortunately, "conference Buddhism" popularizes a very narrow view of Buddhism, which marginalizes or inducts attendees according to the way they fit (or do not) into the perceived agenda. The result is a disservice to those who seek to be genuine practitioners. Such people have purposely tried to water down the Vajrayana teachings for the purpose of making Buddhism neat and tidy for the delicate sensibilities of the therapy generation. It is tragic to witness the fecund, fiery, and feisty spirit with which western people approached the Vajrayana teachings in the 1970s diminishing into a pallid, lackluster bid for security.

We believe that Rig'dzin Dorje's book will provide a voice in the choir of dissident vajra-hope, for the preservation of authentic Vajrayana in the west. We believe that Rig'dzin Dorje's chutzpah will charm those who may have been beguiled by those well-meaning but misguided spokespersons of "conference Buddhism." His enthusiastic honesty provides a counterbalance to the nihilism that has begun to blight the way in which the authentic Vajrayana lineages and their lineage-holders are perceived.

We live at a time when the Vajrayana has become widely available and unusually accessible through books and public teachings—and therein lies a great danger. Buddhism in the west is now not solely taught by eastern teachers but also by their western students. Some of these students have remained true to the essential lineages and teachings, but some seem to have taken refuge in psychotherapy and the paradigm of political correctness. The result of this has been to cause confusion in the minds of those who wish to dedicate their lives to an authentic spiritual endeavor. This is a matter of concern in all schools of Buddhism—but more so within the context of the Vajrayana teachings, as that is the province of the vajra master.

The Role of the Vajra Master

In 1973, Chögyam Trungpa Rinpoche's *Cutting Through Spiritual Materialism* was published (Shambhala Publications). In the twenty-six years that have elapsed, it has remained a classic text that has inspired thousands of western students of Vajrayana. The chapter on the guru from *Cutting Through Spiritual Materialism* is one to which we have repeatedly directed both our own students, and the students of other lamas who have attended our retreats. Among the chief proponents of what we call "politically correct" Buddhism—Buddhism that has been modified by the dictates of what is considered politically correct— are those who only came to hear of the Vajrayana by virtue of the existence of books by Chögyam Trungpa Rinpoche. How sad that the message of this book may be in danger of being casually dismissed by those same people. We are reminded of the Tibetan story of the beggar who used a large lump of gold as a pillow and died of poverty without realizing his great wealth.

In 1976, Chögyam Trungpa Rinpoche again drew our attention to the subject of the vajra master in his book, *The Myth of Freedom* (Shambhala Publications). In this equally brilliant work, he distinguished clearly between the Sutrayana role of spiritual friend and the Vajrayana role of vajra master or "dangerous friend." Yet now we find articles written by individuals who tell us that they "prefer" the term spiritual friend to vajra master—as if it were a matter of personal choice, rather than a matter of the role as it accords with the Buddhist vehicle in question.

The term "dangerous friend" is Trungpa Rinpoche's inspired coinage, and in deference to him we used it in our book *Wearing the Body of Visions* (Aro Books, 1995), as the title of a chapter that discusses the role of the vajra master. Now the term appears again, with our encouragement, as the title of Nga-la Rig'dzin Dorje's first book. This is intended as a statement of profound respect for Trungpa Rinpoche as one of the great Vajrayana masters of the twentieth century.

The role of the *dorje lopön* (rDo rJe sLob dPon), or vajra master, is one with which many proponents of egalitarian western buddhism are uncomfortable. But it should be understood that this is not a question of the incompatibility of an eastern modality with a western context. The proponents of western buddhism would have equal difficulty with the modus operandi of any western military academy, for example. In other words, antipathy to the role of vajra master is not based on the alien quality of an eastern form. If anything, the regimen of a military academy is far more severe than vajra commitment: one is actually physically free to break one's vows and walk away, but one is not physically free to break the terms of military service.

Beyond the question of devotion and surrender being characterized as "mindless obedience," however, there is the question of political correctness and its demand for enforced equality. Political correctness has a built-in demand for equality irrespective of the varied talents of different people. We believe that political correctness is dangerous because it reduces everything down to the lowest common denominator. We hear of western buddhist teachers who advocate dependence on "the collective wisdom of the sangha" as an initiative toward diminishing the role of the lama. In response to this, we would ask what "collective wisdom" might mean in this sense. Could it be said that a hundred thousand dualistic individuals make up one vajra master?

The vajra master sees the enlightened qualities of all his or her disciples, and gives them access to transmission according to their individual capacities and relative constraints. The vajra master loves and appreciates his or her disciples because of their individual neuroses—not in spite of them. Because the beginningless enlightenment of each of us sparkles through the fabric of our neuroses, infinite opportunities for realization exist, as the repertoire of the vajra master's egalitarian effectiveness. Where is the egalitarianism in depriving people of the opportunity to fly beyond the reach and range of their dualistic conditioning? Without the vajra master we are doomed to the slow and painful process of unravelling each minute thread of our tortuous dualistic thinking.

Political Correctness and Egalitarianism

Rig'dzin Dorje has risen to the challenge of warning people against the fascist undercurrents of political correctness. Vajrayana has no political bias—its frame of reference lies completely beyond the dictates that govern the ordinary ordering of society. Vajrayana does not deny the validity of democracy or egalitarianism within secular society. Vajrayana simply speaks of the natural right to be free—even to the extent of being free of the myth of freedom.

Vajrayana presents vajra relationship with the lama as the final portal of freedom. Through this portal we enter a dimension in which we can question the otherwise unquestionable—our narcissistic determination to maintain the illusion of duality. Those who seem most afraid of the vajra master would appear to be those who are most afraid of acknowledging the extent of their own narcissism.

Vajrayana holds that everyone is equal in terms of our intrinsic vajra nature—our beginningless enlightenment. Vajrayana holds that all beings are equally worthy of compassion. However, Vajrayana does not hold that beings should be restricted in their capacity according to the lowest common denominator allowed by those who wish to curtail human freedom. To restrict people's freedom to make value judgments in order to enforce an artificial equality is to shrink the quality of life.

Relationship with a vajra master is not democratic. This may appear somewhat shocking, but we need to understand that our relationship with reality is also not democratic. There is no tribunal to which we can appeal when our lover leaves us, or when the weather becomes unseasonably hot. Vajra commitment and vajra relationship cannot be crudely compared with political totalitarianism.

Even if democracy were such a wonderful phenomenon—where do we authentically find democracy in the world? Every "democratic" society would appear to be ruled by powerful influential factors that attempt to remain discreet. Within every democracy we find dictatorship manifesting under the guise of consensus.

Neither democracy nor totalitarianism offers real freedom—and neither has anything in common with vajra relationship. From the perspective of Vajrayana, dictators are no freer than those to whom they dictate. Theft of individual freedom has been perpetrated by representatives of the broad spectrum of political philosophies, so there is no guarantee that any conventional point of view can create a sane compassionate society.

Obsession with individual freedom at the expense of others is the death of compassion. Obsession with neurotic parental-style control at the expense of the personal liberty of others is the death of wisdom. We can never be free of freedom—if freedom is our obsession. If we cannot be free to give up the sovereignty of our narcissistic rational, Vajrayana becomes meaningless. If we fail to recognize the compassionate nature of vajra relationship as the heart of Vajrayana, then we are left merely with a prosaic esoteric pastime.

Certain western scholars have put forth the idea that the answer lies in the texts rather than the vajra master. But Yeshé Tsogyel herself, when imploring Padmasambhava not to leave Tibet, cried: "For Tibet a time of inky darkness has arrived, when people hope instruction can be found in books."

The vajra master holds the lineage of the essential meaning, and without the vajra master, one is merely left with dead information. But these scholars have asserted that freedom lies in the capacity to read texts in their original languages—as if transmission were merely a question of intellectual comprehension, and liberation a matter of having gathered sufficient information. Such scholars, far from being the liberators of an enslaved spiritual proletariat, would merely create an intellectual elite who would eventually hold dominion over those for whom the intellect was not a prime sense field.

The spurious academic approach simply sets up its own hierarchy. With this method, only those with a privileged social background, superior intellectual endowment, and independent financial resources can become authentic practitioners. This can hardly be described as egalitarian. When one penetrates such sham egalitarianism, it becomes clear that the vajra master is actually the means by which the broadest spectrum of human beings have access to the Vajrayana. It is therefore the vajra master who provides the truest and most universal egalitarian context.

Crazy Wisdom

The role of vajra master in the context of "crazy wisdom" (*yeshé cholwa*; *ye shes chol ba*), is particularly repugnant to some who claim to be politically correct, but it is also a role with which some strains of institutionalism are equally uneasy. In 1991, Chögyam Trungpa Rinpoche's *Crazy Wisdom* (Shambhala Publications) was published, and we were treated to the most masterful exposition of this glorious form of transmission. Even in Tibet such perspectives were closely guarded, so the wide accessibility of this material in the west should have provided a basis from which the practice of Vajrayana could have gained strength and conviction. It is sad to think that many of those who now criticize the role of the vajra master are also those who have had the opportunity to read this magnificent work.

With regard to the historical context of crazy wisdom, there were even a few institutions in Tibet where the display of miracles (*ngodrüp* or *siddhis*) was cause for expulsion, a fact that indicates that religious institutions often exist for their own perpetuation rather than to facilitate realization. Most religions prefer to venerate saints who are safely dead. They prefer their ecclesiastics to conform to recognizable legislated codes—even though the realization expressed by mystics of all religions has always gone beyond the boundaries of ossified hierarchic sanction.

The spiritual stories that actually inspire people are those which concern enlightened masters who expressed freedom from the conventional norms, including religious norms: Padmasambhava, Yeshé Tsogyel, Tilopa, Naropa, Marpa, Milarépa, Shri Simha, Drukpa Künlegs, Dokhyentsé Yeshé Dorje, Dungsé Thrinlé Norbu Rinpoche, Kyabjé Künzag Dorje Rinpoche, Jomo Sam'phel, and Chögyam Trungpa Rinpoche. These masters and others like them are the ones we look to for inspiration.

The initial phase of Vajrayana in the west was welcomed by the chaotic ethos of the 1960s which, however chemically befuddled, provided an atmosphere of freedom and open-mindedness. In contrast, the 1980s and 1990s have been characterized by the rise of neo-Puritanism, and the mode of crazy wisdom has been demonized by those whose spirituality is dominated by concepts of political correctness. western style "conference dharma" has sought to issue legislation as to what is acceptable and what is unacceptable according to the dictates of psychotherapy. Such conferences have expressed enthusiasm for establishing historical limits as to what was "real Buddhism" and what were "later digressions," (by which they mean Vajrayana Buddhism). The creation of strict demarcations appears to be more important than celebrating wider horizons of possibility. It would seem that conferences have occurred throughout history in many religions, but one thing is certain: whenever committees cast votes as to what is authentic, authenticity is likely to be found elsewhere. In such dismal times as these, it is marvellous to know of a person such as Nga-la Rig'dzin Dorje and to read his excellent book.

We are fortunate in the west that the mahasiddha Chögyam Trungpa Rinpoche left a legacy of teachings, in fluent contemporary English, which provide a powerful vision of the heart of Vajrayana. Dungsé Thrinlé Norbu Rinpoche has also written works of outstanding brilliance in English—and to him we owe an immense debt of gratitude. Other lamas have left western-language legacies of great inspiration, and many continue to dedicate their lives to this end. Those who have received transmissions and taken empowerments should not betray this legacy for false promises made on the basis of a fundamentally nihilistic utopianism. Those who are interested in Buddhism, of whatever school, should look carefully and intelligently at what is being propounded. There are glorious traditions with unbroken lineages to which we owe our opportunities for freedom, and those who break their vows to these lineages in order to fabricate something new should not seek to inveigle others with fraudulent home-grown doctrines of sanitized teachings. Those with an unclouded appreciation of manifest Vajrayana will know clearly that Chögyam Trungpa Rinpoche illuminated the very core of what is possible in terms of crazy wisdom.

Western yogis such as Rig'dzin Dorje are rare, particularly in his native country of England. Books such as this are valuable, and we are grateful to him for the work he has put into completing this text. We felt it was crucial that this book should appear at this time to stand as a testament and a validation of the authentic lama-disciple relationship.

Rig'dzin Dorje's training as a lama in the Aro gTér lineage of the Nyingma tradition has been no different (at the external level) from which we ourselves experienced. We could not, of course, provide him with the inspiration of our own vajra masters; we are merely the inconsequential eccentrics with whom Rig'dzin Dorje has taken vows of vajra commitment. That he accepts us as vajra masters is due to his own enthusiasm for the Vajrayana teachings of Padmasambhava and Yeshé Tsogyel, and for the gTérmas of Khyungchen Aro Lingma, rather than for any qualities we might be said to possess. Because of his own qualities, and due to his immense diligence, we gave him ngak'phang ordination in 1990 and authorized him to accept his own students as a lama of the lineage. Nga-la Rig'dzin Dorje is a resolute and passionate practitioner who maintains the white skirt and uncut hair of the gö-kar-chang-lo'i-dé (*go dKar lCang lo'i sDe*) tradition with rare aplomb. He now inspires others with his clear-headed devotion and commitment. His commitment has always been based on serious study, practice, and retreat experience. He is a practitioner who knows the meaning of refuge, unlike those who take refuge in whatever the strong feeling of the moment happens to be on the basis of having followed the dictates of and infantile narcissistic impulse. He is a yogi who has applied himself acutely within the felt dimension of informal symbolic transmission, and is thus well-qualified to write a book such as this.

Ngak'chang Chö-ying Gyamtso and
Khandro Déchen Tsédrüp Rolpa'i Yeshé

Aro Taktsang, Penarth, Wales
November 1999

INTRODUCTION

Buddhist Traditions and Vehicles

Buddhism is a multifaceted revelation of the non-dual state. Although it is usually the "religions of the Book," the theistic religions (Judaism, Christianity, and Islam), which people think of as having been revealed (by a creator deity), Buddhism can also be described as a revealed religion. With Buddhism, particularly Vajrayana Buddhism, is the revelation of our inherent enlightened nature. That is the manner of expression of the gTérma lineages of the Nyingma tradition especially.

Vajrayana is the efflorescence of the *sambhogakaya,* the dimension of indestructible energy, and therefore by nature is a revelation of vision. The Buddhist understanding of enlightenment views the non-dual state as the actual nature of all living beings, rather than as a gift from without. No concept of a creator god has ever emerged from an authentic Buddhist tradition, and it is only now, at the turn of the twenty-first century, that we witness so-called western buddhist teachers attempting to exempt the concept of the creator god from the Buddhist critique, which has always rejected it as eternalistic monism, or eternalistic dualism.

So, through revelation in the Buddhist sense, descriptions of the path to enlightenment from the vision and experience of realized teachers have unfolded many times in history. For Buddhists, the different explanations of how to understand enlightenment, and the teachings that go with them, have always tended to reflect the great differences in the times, places and cultures in which they arose. They resemble travel directions to a single destination, but written from the perspective of setting out from a variety of widely separated points. In similar fashion, any Buddhist book is also implicitly a statement of difference, not necessarily in the spirit of argument, but simply by virtue of being highly particular.

The various Buddhist traditions can be strikingly divergent, to the extent that they sometimes appear to contradict each other in key areas. Even these remarks have the flavor of one particular strand of Buddhism. This is the view that stems from the culture of the eighty-four mahasiddhas, and is also reflective of the personal traditions that came from Padmasambhava and Yeshe Tsogyel,[1] the Tantric Buddhas in Tibet, who were heirs of the mahasiddhas. Similarly, the meditation lineage later passed from the mahasiddhas Tilopa and Naropa, into Tibet through Marpa, to Marpa's non-monastic disciple Milarépa and his disciple Réchungpa. To describe all this simply as Tibetan Buddhism would be to detract from its inherence within a vast Buddhist continuum, which has flowed unbroken from about 400 BCE through to this century, and from Asia to the rest of the world.

Mandarava was an Indian princess, but she accepted the wandering, supposedly disreputable yogi Padmasambhava as both teacher and consort, even in face of death threats from her father. Naropa was an eminent professor, but he submitted to ordeals of purification at the direction of his teacher Tilopa, who was a person completely outside and antipathetic to any issues of social nicety. Milarépa, a near-penniless, uneducated refugee from both justice and injustice, lived in the house of his teacher Marpa, who was by occupation a wealthy farmer as well as being much sought-after as a lama, and the pre-eminent scholar-translator of his age. When Milarépa, a non-celibate, illiterate hermit living entirely on charity, became famous as a teacher himself, one of his most important disciples was the monk Gampopa, who was also a doctor. Such a proliferation of diverse relationships made any notion of conformity or uniformity inoperative, while at the same time eliminating any grounds for contradiction or conflict. Not for nothing has this been described as a golden age.

Although all these masters and their lineages are still hugely celebrated in Vajrayana Buddhism and in Tibetan popular culture, this was never the dominant format of religious activity in Tibet, nor did it aspire to be. The style of the mahasiddhas always retained a quality of the Indian Buddhist tradition, of being free of the caste system, outside the social structure altogether. In Tibet there is a proverb: "Every valley has a unique dialect, every Lama has a unique teaching."

Some of these paths have been effective for thousands of years. The most famous examples are the Sutric teachings of the Prince of the Shakya clan, Siddhartha Gautama, the Buddha of the historical era. This tradition is mainly—but not entirely—renunciate, celibate, monastic, and intellectual. By contrast, the Vajrayana tradition of the mahasiddhas is non-monastic, non-celibate, and non-institutional. It practices gender equality or even prioritizes the status of women, and embraces every conceivable kind of lifestyle as spiritual practice in itself. Tantric practitioners recognized their personal teacher as the summation of all religious and secular authority, irrespective of social or other status on either side. Even within the monastic hierarchy, there is no court of appeal beyond the vajra master. This was clearly demonstrated when a number of the western students of the late Gélugpa Lama Geshé Rabten made a deputation to His Holiness Dala'i Lama about their growing feelings of incompatibility with Geshé Rabten's traditional teaching style. However, His Holiness Dala'i Lama firmly declined to intervene between them and their personal teacher.

Although some Buddhist paths have been appreciated for centuries across subcontinents, other paths of practice have been known to no more than a few hundred or even a few score people living in one remote locality. These differences of scale have no relevance at all to the superiority or inferiority of these teachings, or to their future durability. From within central Tibet, four of the mightiest rivers in Asia have their beginnings: the Indus, the Brahmaputra, the Yangtze, and the Mekong. All of them begin as rivulets that one might step over without noticing. By contrast, in the same mountains there are impressive torrents that thunderously divide the valleys, only to plummet without warning through the jaws of a cavern into fathomless irredeemable obscurity. Let the "stream-enterer" beware . . .[2]

It is worth remembering some examples from our own cultural history. Christianity in Europe began as a religion adopted by the disenfranchised, which in those days meant mostly slaves and women. They met in secret and had a short time frame; they imminently expected the return of their messiah. No one at that time would have predicted that the most powerful center of Christianity would one day be a palace, an independent city-state, decorated by the greatest artists in the history of the subcontinent, patronized by emperors, located in the heart of that very same city, with a time frame of millennia. Likewise no one in the present day should judge the hugely diverse coexisting Buddhist traditions by criteria of worldly success that are not regarded as relevant by Buddhism itself.

In Tibet, during the second spread of the Buddhist teachings, the cultural ethos seemed to move more in the direction of centralized authority, formalized spiritual hierarchy, scholastic achievement, and social order. A new, more institutional style of Buddhist practice evolved, different in flavor to that of the first spread of Buddhism in Tibet. This new style was a spiritual synthesis, a hybrid that incorporated Tantric practice within a Sutric framework. By Sutric, in this context, I mean avowedly renunciate, ideally the lifestyle of a monastic. By Tantric I mean the style of practice typified by the mahasiddhas, in which ordinary psychology and emotions are liberated in the process

4

of actively embracing them just as they are. The energy and intensity of their manifestations are respected as the most powerful fuel of practice.

Containing Tantra within Sutra is akin to the setup of a nuclear fusion reactor, in which a magnetic field (the monastic vows) prevents the inconceivably high temperatures of the fusion reaction (Tantric practice) from destroying the container-vessel (the ordinary mind of the practitioner, and the hierarchic institution itself). Every religious initiative in Tibetan history thereafter has represented a new amalgam of a similar kind. Different vehicles of Buddhist practice are characterized by different styles of manifesting the role of teacher. The definition of "vehicle" is that it possesses a base, path, and fruit (or result).[3] The base is the experience, understanding, or personal development of the practitioner—one's actual condition. The path is the type of practice appropriate for that condition. The fruit is the accomplishment or fulfillment of the path. Each vehicle contains its own foundation (preliminary practice, or *ngöndro*), which is designed to bring the practitioner to the required base. Ngöndro is always composed of exercises consistent with the style of the vehicle, in the same way that training for a sport naturally makes intensive use of particulars of the sport itself.

Classifying Buddhism according to vehicles is mainly characteristic of Tibetan or trans–Himalayan Buddhism. This is complicated by the fact that there are at least four different methods of making such a classification, which are used by different schools, and even sometimes within particular vehicles and particular schools. The simplest method of classification comes from the Dzogchen perspective of the Nyingma tradition, which is regarded as the highest teaching.[4] This view divides Buddhist practice into Sutra, Tantra, and Dzogchen, and describes them according to principle as follows:

Sutra is characterized as the path of renunciation, in the sense of rejecting every kind of form to which one might develop attachment. The Sutric teacher is the perfect 'spiritual friend' (Tib. *gewa'i shenyen* – *dGe ba'i gShes gNyan*; Skt. *kalyana mitra*), a monk or nun who is utterly reliable, and open to being evaluated exactly according to the *vinaya* of monastic discipline and the bodhisattva vows.

Tantra is characterized as the path of transformation, in the sense of making use of every kind of form that arises, especially one's own psycho-physical and emotional experience. The Tantric teacher is the vajra master (Tib. *dorje lopön* – rDo rJe bLo dPon; Skt. *vajra charya*), the teacher who manifests the teachings through the symbolic wealth and richness of his or her display of personality.[5]

Dzogchen is characterized as the path of self-liberation, in that all perception and experience has the nature of liberation of itself. The Dzogchen teacher is also the vajra master, but here he or she spontaneously transmits the realized state without the need of any intermediate symbolism or ritual to those who are open to receiving it completely unmediated.

Ngak'chang Rinpoche and Khandro Déchen, in a letter to their disciples, describe the distinction as follows:

> Sutra is the path of renunciation—because the principle and function of Sutra concerns the way in which we manipulate the world of form as a series of potential reference points through which we hope to establish ourselves as solid, permanent, separate, continuous and defined entities. Due to our manipulative relationship with form, we renounce it in favour of emptiness and do so through a wide variety of methods which reflect emptiness.
>
> Tantra is the path of transformation—because the principle and function of Tantra concerns our beginningless enlightened nature in terms of how it becomes distorted through dualism. Every dualistic mind-set is actually a symbol of the enlightened state through an intrinsic energetic connection. In Tantra, therefore, every dualistic neurosis is open to the process of transformation through the path of symbol. The vajra master becomes indispensable—as a living symbol of our own enlightened state.

Dzogchen is the path of self-liberation—because the principle and function of Dzogchen concerns the beginningless enlightened state in terms of its inherent self-existent naturalness. Whatever arises from emptiness can therefore liberate itself simply through its own arising—nothing more is required. In Dzogchen, therefore, whatever dualistic tendency appears to manifest is open to relaxing into its own condition through the power of the transmission we receive from the vajra master—the one who continually reflects our primordial state of enlightenment.

Understanding the different Buddhist teachings requires different cognitive tools. To understand Sutra, one needs an ordinary mind. It doesn't have to be a brilliant mind, just good enough. To understand Tantra, one needs to know the empty state. Then one can understand form in terms of its empty nature. In Dzogchen the cognitive tool is *rigpa*—empty awareness having the quality of knowing without any subject or object: it cognizes itself. One does not need the experience of rigpa to understand the Four Naljors (the foundation teachings of Dzogchen *sem-dé*), but it is necessary for integration with the sensory experiences generated in Dzogchen *long-dé*.[6] And in the case of Dzogchen *men-ngag-dé*, one cannot even approach the practice unless one can receive the instructions in the state of rigpa.

Buddha Shakyamuni predicted that the community of his Sutric practitioners would last for only five hundred years in a form that would not have to be re-interpreted by realized masters according to the prevailing cultural milieu. But he predicted that the Tantric Buddhist teachings would endure for fifty thousand years. The Dzogchen teachings are beyond time. Ngak'chang Rinpoche explained to me personally that

The Buddhist yanas or vehicles, can be categorized in various ways according to tradition—but in terms of the Dzogchen view, we divide them according to the kayas, or spheres of being. Sutra, which is comprised of Shravakabuddhayana, Pratyékabuddhayana, and Bodhisattvabuddhayana, belongs to the sphere of realized manifestation—trülku or nirmanakaya. Vajrayana, which is comprised of tantra and Dzogchen, belongs to the sphere of realised appearance and the sphere of unconditioned potentiality—long-ku or sambhogakaya and chö-ku or dharmakaya, respectively. Sutra, Tantra, and Dzogchen are therefore temporally linked with the kayas. Sutra, being linked with the nirmanakaya, is of shorter applicable duration than Tantra, which is linked with the sambhogakaya. And Dzogchen, being linked with dharmakaya, is endless. There is nothing to change and nothing which changes within the emptiness of vajra nature.

If we look at Buddhism in the western world today, it is the Sutric teachings that are most widely known and understood. This is because they are the most accessible to the intellect, even though they relate primarily to a lifestyle of celibate mendicancy. The Tantric teachings are becoming fairly well known and widely published, but not always in terms which adequately reflect their qualities. And the Dzogchen teachings could be said to have been realized in inverse proportion to the *succès d'estime* that they have achieved in popular appreciation.

Evaluating Buddhist traditions without actually practicing them is a thoroughly useless pursuit. It is liable to decline into one of two fallacies, which I call the "historicist" fallacy and the "essentialist" fallacy. The former tends toward scholasticism or sectarianism, the latter more toward populism and "new age" spiritual materialism.

The historicist fallacy is to recognize only certain styles, phases, or geographical disseminations of Buddhism as "authentic," meaning transmissions of teachings that a practitioner could follow to enlightenment. I was once shocked to hear a number of western buddhist teachers propose that there should be a "cutoff date" for authentically "Buddhist" teachings, with anything after that being considered "not kosher." This concept undermines the very idea of enlighten......... itself as an experience of "as it is" and turns Buddhism into a dead tradition of articles of faith and received wisdom. If followed to its logical conclusion, it would eventually come to question how much confidence one might have even in the personal experience of the historical Buddha.

The essentialist fallacy is to declare all Buddhist teachings to be of equal value to all practitioners. Although this sounds admirably open-minded, it is an equally destructive tendency. Different strands of Buddhist teaching have always been aimed at individuals of differing capacity, experience and personality. That is why so many different teachings exist, to communicate with different varieties of practitioner. Those who say, "it's all essentially the same so it doesn't matter which practice/teacher/sangha/school," are never able to develop an enduring commitment to any particular path.

These paradoxes perfectly reflect the teaching of the *Prajnaparamita Sutra*. In this Sutra, Avalokiteshvara says "Form is emptiness; emptiness is form. Emptiness is not other than form, form none other than emptiness." This may sound impenetrable, but, according to the Tibetan system, the *Prajnaparamita Sutra*, correctly understood, is a key to every Buddhist path. All other Buddhist teachings could be considered as its commentary and footnotes. The idea is that, although both beings and phenomena have a real appearance (form), they have no essential nature that can be discovered (emptiness).

In the realized state, form and emptiness are not perceived as being separate. Although they both continue to manifest, one is not conditioned by either of them. They move, alternate, flow, or dance, and the practitioner experiences no obstacle, difference, friction, or separation. When one knows that "single experience" for oneself, then form and emptiness are "not two" any longer; they become the ever-changing decorations of the one experience. This would be the view of Prajnaparamita from the perspective of realized experience, in the style of Dzogchen.

Both the historicist and the essentialist fallacies try to separate emptiness and form. This always turns out to be a hopeless endeavor because whichever aspect one emphasizes, it can only be experienced in its relationship with the other. The historicist fallacy tries to pin down form and thereby deadens it. The essentialist fallacy, by contrast, grasps at the essential sameness (emptiness) of all forms, ignoring their particularity and focus, which results in a bland statement that, "everything is everything." As practitioners, it is our responsibility to find the Middle Way of commitment to the practice, teacher, and lineage that we choose on the basis of what is appropriate to our actual condition.

A lineage of a thousand years exists in its entirety only in the dimension of vision. One visualizes the lineage in meditation, during full-length prostrations, with its culmination in the person of one's own lama. That vision does not alter when the student becomes a teacher and receives prostrations in turn from a new generation of students. In the face of the generations of unimaginably great teachers who have preceded the new student, he or she feels utterly inconsequential and is thrown into the empty state. But here is a paradox: without this student, it is the previous generations that are as nothing. Without their heir in the present day, their influence would cease. The lineage is form, the student is emptiness; also, the student is form, the lineage is emptiness. The two aspects flicker, reflect each other, and implore to be perceived as immaculately related. The newest student, making prostrations as the first exercise in the Tantric foundation practices, is offered this perfect introduction to non-duality. The frictionless inseparability of teacher and student in this visionary dimension becomes a metaphor. In the dimension of Mind (I am defining *Mind* with an uppercase *M* as ordinary mind that has recognized its beginninglessly enlightened wisdom nature) it is the realization of referenceless non-duality. In the dimension of the habitable world, it is compassionate activity, which undertakes to spread the teachings to everyone and everything everywhere.

I

OPENING

The relationship between the vajra master and vajra student should be the most important relationship in one's life as a spiritual aspirant. This is the only relationship we can have which ultimately leads to enlightenment. From the Vajrayana point of view it is more important than our relationship with our spouse, our children, or our parents. For a Vajrayana student it is more important than this one life.

"Without the vajra master, there is no Vajrayana." These were the words of my vajra masters, and the words of their vajra masters. These words might well have been expressed through the lineage of non-dual experience for two thousand years, but it is only in the west, and at the turn of the twentieth century, that they have needed to be expressed. It is only in this time and this place that we need to define the essence of Vajrayana in order to demonstrate that the role of vajra master is indispensable.

The vajra master provides the fuel for the path. Without fuel, engines are curios to be preserved in the museums of cultures which have depleted their fuel supplies, and no longer have recourse to motorized transportation. Ngak'chang Rinpoche and Khandro Déchen, in a vajra letter to their sangha, made this clear:

Petrol or gasoline may well be dermatologically harmful, but without it one's Harley Davidson or Vincent Black Lightning can only roll down convenient hills. One can strip a vehicle down and expose the engine in the creation of a dragster, but if one removes parts of the engine, even the most luxurious sedan will not serve its intended purpose. The vajra master is the living fuel of Vajrayana—of Tantra and of Dzogchen—and politically correct, "psycho-egalitarian" arguments as to the unsuitability of this mode for the western temperament are both fatuous and flaccid.

Our experience of emptiness or devotion is the base; realization of the nature of Mind is the fruit or result. But the vajra master is the path. It was Trungpa Rinpoche who coined the memorable description of the Tantric teacher as "the dangerous friend"; dangerous because the student grants the lama a dramatic freedom of action. Khandro Déchen, in answer to a question I asked, confided the following:

> The vajra master is dangerous in the sense of the danger a vacuum cleaner poses to a carpet, or that a bath poses to body odour. The Lama is dangerous to our dualistic conceptions—but beyond that, he or she is the compassionate surgeon who saves our lives. The surgeon's knife cuts us open—but if there's a cancer to be removed, then the operation is to be welcomed.

"New age" spirituality in general is afraid of danger, as is the society that spawned it. Nowadays people seek guarantees about aspects of life that were previously treated as matters of individual responsibility. There is a little fishing village in Cornwall, England where a diving board has been removed on the grounds that people might dive in at low tide and hurt themselves. In some ways it is laudable that people wish to protect others—but the result of this kind of paternalism is that we are gradually stripped of more and more sense of personal responsibility. This actually has the effect of making us more vulnerable—rather than protecting us through encouraging greater responsibility. So those who say that association with the vajra master is unacceptably perilous are also saying that the individual is incapable of making choices which involve risk. Would they also wish to legislate against skiing, parachuting, and climbing trees? Many people in the world take calculated risks and are admired for their adventurous spirit. But when the "politically correct" discuss the role of the vajra master, they seem unwilling to allow individuals the right to chose— even though their choices are regulated by warnings that are as ancient as the role itself. The person who leads an Outward Bound weekend pushes people to overcome their limitations in terms of rock climbing or some other physical pursuit. The lama as vajra master pushes us beyond our dualistic rationale. Ngak'chang Rinpoche says of the vajra master in this context:

> The Lama is the ecstatic, wild, and gentle figure who short-circuits your systems of self-referencing. The Lama is the only person in your life who cannot be manipulated. The Lama is the invasion of unpredictability you allow into your life, to enable you to cut through the convolutions of interminable psychological and emotional processes. The Lama is the terrifyingly compassionate gamester who re-shuffles the deck of your carefully arranged rationale.[1] To enter into vajra commitment is to leap from the perfect precipice. To find yourself in the radiant space of this choiceless choice, is the very heart of Tantra. To leap open-eyed into the shining emptiness of the Lama's wisdom display, and to experience the ecstatic impact of each dynamic gesture of the Lama's method display is the essential luminosity and power of the path.[2]

In Tibetan Buddhism we take refuge in Guru (lama; *b La ma*), Buddha (sang-gyé; *sangs rGyas*), Dharma (chö; *chos*), and Sangha (gendün; *dGe dun*). This is an acknowledgment that it is only through the energy, kindness, and activity of the lama that Buddha, Dharma, and Sangha can be accessed. A personal relationship with a lama is absolutely necessary for Tantric practice to have any function whatsoever. The relationship between the lama, or vajra master, and vajra student should be the most important relationship in one's life as a spiritual aspirant. This is the only relationship we can have that ultimately leads to enlightenment. From the Vajrayana point of view it is more important than our relationship with our spouse, our children, or our parents. For a Vajrayana student it is more important than this one life.

The primary goal of Tantric practice is to experience the relationship between form and emptiness as non-duality. This is called *ro-chig*, "the one taste." The vajra master embodies that realization in person. But this experience, because it is non-dual, neither belongs nor does not belong to the teacher as an individual: it was neither born with anyone nor does it ever die with anyone. Whenever this state is experienced by one being, it can also be experienced by others, mutually and simultaneously, without having to be conceptualized as something that travels between one party and another, like spooky vibes wobbling through the twilight zone. It is called transmission; realization as an outlook shared by individuals. If one could experience the mind of the lama oneself, enter that unconditioned condition, then that would constitute one's own experience of the realized state. This "unifying with the mind of the lama" is the fruit of the practice of guru yoga (lama'i naljor; *bLa ma'i rNal 'Byor*), which is the essential practice of Vajrayana. All the traditional stipulations about the teacher-student relationship in Vajrayana are founded on this prospect, even though to Buddhists of other persuasions it might sound incomprehensible.

The coming together of lama and student at this level is called vajra relationship or vajra commitment. This Tantric expression refers to the relationship with a root teacher or *tsa-wa'i lama* (Tib. *rTsa ba'i bLa ma*, Skt. *Mula Guru*) which is beyond the possibility of being broken by either party. The root teacher is the lama whose realization enables one to experience the nature of Mind. The symbolism of a root is that if the root is cut, the tree dies. One would never wish to be cut off from one's root teacher. One aspires to remain in a state of continuous transmission, just as the life of a tree is sustained by its roots' capacity to draw up water. The life of the tree and the life of one's practice depend upon the root. Without the root there is no water and no life. Without the root teacher there is no transmission, and no enlightenment.

The method of the root teacher or vajra master is traditionally compared to a mirror. Much has been written in Buddhist literature about the mirror-like qualities of realization. Using the mirror as a traditional metaphor for the mind, the mirror reflects anything that appears, in the same way as the senses perceive whatever arises. But the reflections in the mirror neither define the mirror nor disturb it in the slightest. An image from the Dzogchen teachings has the mirror facing both ways: Mind (emptiness) reflects phenomena (form) while phenomena are also a mirror that reflects Mind. The sky of the nature of Mind and the space of phenomena have the same quality—the one taste.

The contrasting view, which we try to maintain in ordinary mind, is that the world and ourselves are separate containers with their contents. This is how we try to preserve our sense of limited identity, without ever asking ourselves why it is that restricted identity should seem more valuable than the unpartitioned mind-space of realization. Tantra brings the functioning of all the senses, in both their penetrating accuracy and their absorbing enthusiasm, into the path of practice. Tantra empowers every style of creativity to be a carrier of symbolism. Transmission could be given through an artistic process that pertained to any or every sense faculty. It could be scented in the tonifying aroma of medically formulated incense, felt in the stinging shower of sparks from vajra weapons being sharpened, heard in the thud of a hopelessly blunt chopper mangling the meat for *mo-mos*[3] on a slab of tree-trunk in a kitchen-hovel by the gloom of a hurricane lamp.[4] Or it could be the gemlike display and clear, separate flavors of the food offerings representing the five elements for the *tsog* feast.

In the realized state, mind and space are connected, non-dual, and they are interfaced at the threshold of the senses. Realized experience is constantly moving backward and forward across this threshold in an unending, unbroken play of smooth alternation—now one, now the other. This is a single experience, but is sometimes ornamented by oneself reflected in the mirror of phenomena, and sometimes ornamented by phenomena reflected in the mirror of Mind. Sometimes one aspect is form and the other is emptiness, sometimes the other way around. When these two interchange without the slightest sense of interruption, of duality, then this constitutes the manifestation of rigpa, the non-dual state.[5] At this point the analogy of the mirror dissolves into itself and disappears: even this mirror is ultimately empty.

The mirror of the lama reflects both the quality of our enlightenment and the style of our unenlightenment, such that we are able to recognize them both. That means on the one hand being able to tell them apart, but also being able to glimpse the dimension in which they interlock. This coming to recognition is understood to be both a long and a gradual process. But it could also be completely accomplished in a moment, or in many moments from time to time, like a stroboscope that accelerates in frequency. There might be occasional glimmers of accomplishing the whole path at once, in an instantaneous process; and in the next moment being unable to find it again, or unable even to say anything cogent about it. The power of karmic vision[6] draws us back again and again into our own personal style of incomprehension. But overall the student experiences the density and gravity of ordinary personality clearing and dissolving into a pulsing energetic display of form and emptiness. Personality can no longer be assumed to be real. One's experience of having a self becomes somewhat like an interference pattern that is created in the moment by the incoherence of neurosis resonating with the coherence of clarity. As Ngak'chang Rinpoche puts it:

The sense in which existence and non-existence can be said to flicker on the brink of entry into vajra relationship, is when you're able to lose track of who you are. You find yourself defined only in the moment; or for that matter, undefined in the moment. There can exist a sense of emptiness; of personal transparency in which "what you are" is quite mutable. This flickering is the sensation in which attachment to personal definition dissolves—it is overawed by the presence of the Lama.[7]

The vajra master, who knows this state, is the mirror itself, emptiness in person, and this empty mirror is turned on the empty student. The student aspires to unite with the teacher in the dimension of the quality of Mind—realization. This is guru yoga. In practicing guru yoga what the student is doing, in effect, is empowering the teacher to be the form quality of the relationship, while the student's sense of self dissolves into emptiness. When that process is successful, the student is able to experience merging with that which the mirror indicates: the realized state. This is all that exists in the teacher's empty mirror-like perception of the student's fundamental nature.

My experience of my tsa-wa'i lamas, Ngak'chang Rinpoche and Khandro Déchen, has always been intensely inspirational. From the start I sensed a vastness, a further horizon, a space of experience that I had not previously known or even imagined. But perhaps I had been longing for it without being aware of it because there was also a sense of familiarity, of recognition, of coming home. In the years that I have known them and studied with them, this has continued to deepen. Those who fear the role of vajra student as being subservient need only witness the immense devotion that their teachers express in turn toward their own lamas in order to realize the empowering nature of this devotion. Ngak'chang Rinpoche and Khandro Déchen speak of Kyabjé Künzang Dorje Rinpoche and Jomo Sam'phel so often and with such joy that the living thread of lineage is palpably demonstrated. Their own power is enhanced rather than diminished by the wholehearted respect they have for their teachers. Ngak'chang Rinpoche and Khandro Déchen have said to me of devotion:

> Those who are afraid of devotion, or who find themselves politi-cally offended by this wisdom-emotion, would appear to lack a crucial understanding of the relationship between anyone and that which they perceive as valuable. One is always in a devotional relationship with anything one prizes—be it a painting, a sculp-ture, a lover—anything or anyone irreplaceable. If one abjures devotion on the grounds of disdain for obsequiousness, one ren-ders oneself unable to appreciate, and therefore unable to enjoy or delight in anything at all. Devotion which resembles obse-quiousness is not wisdom-emotion—but rather a self-serving strategy based on the misconception that one can seduce the vajra master with servile behaviour. One experiences wisdom-emotion with regard to the vajra master simply because one experiences their congruence with the non-dual state, and the inordinate value of this.
>
> Our devotion for Kyabjé Künzang Dorje Rinpoche and Jomo Sam'phel bases itself on how they embody this state.

It is natural that the student's experience of this ability in the lama should inspire confidence. Ultimate experience generates confidence that gradually proves itself unshakable. Vajra relationship is regarded as making enlightenment, at some point, in some lifetime, inevitable. This is why vajra relationship becomes the foundation of a commit-ment that is more than lifelong. Sealed by vows that function at the level of the nature of Mind itself, this relationship empowers a karmic persistence for life after life, until complete realization is attained. In this certainty, the student meanwhile offers the teacher complete freedom to use any of the means of compassionate manipulation, the liberated karmas of the buddhas—enriching, pacifying, magne-tizing, and destroying—to bring the student to that ultimate point.

However, if the student struggles with the process of letting go of the form of self, the mirror of the lama becomes more interactive. It reveals the superficial structure of the student's neurosis, but from angles that cannot be manipulated according to vanity. This "interference pattern" then heats up with friction. Ironically, the friction is generated by the student applying neurotic evasions onto neurotic evasions, the self-torture of dividing against oneself in order to remain wedded to unenlightenment. It is all hideously circular, because unenlightenment is solely and simply this very process. But in the presence of the lama, active neurosis and the active denial of neurosis are forced to collide and implode, like matter meeting anti-matter, and this can momentarily land the student on the groundless ground of ordinary mind; great Mind, the nature of Mind—which is enlightenment itself.

2

APPROACHING THE TIGER

Once we perceive the small space of our habitual mind, we begin to long for the open vastness we have glimpsed in the eyes of the lama. We begin to understand that in "giving up" the dubious freedom of following our dualistic rationale, we are in fact losing nothing and gaining the possibility of everything.

Choosing a lama is not unlike choosing a lifelong marital partner. It is a choice in which one should exercise great care, great seriousness, and great passion. Yet at the beginning of one's interest in spirituality, the choice of a teacher can also reflect decision modes that are as ordinary as choosing a respectable suit of clothing. One must cut one's cloth according to one's means; which in this context would be applying open-hearted intelligence and utilizing the ground of experience to find out exactly who the lama might be, as an extraordinary human being. In terms of clothing, we have to learn to distinguish between sloppily thrown together fashion *schmatas* and the elegant dignity of a classical form, or any variety of well-crafted apparel. Discriminating in this way is a positive exercise in which we learn more about ourselves, while at the same time beginning to wear out the intellectual "muscles" that maintain our judgemental, self-gratifying, supercilious view. We begin to relax into experience.

An interesting example, in terms of the analogy of clothing, relates to the dress style of my teacher, Ngak'chang Rinpoche. When he is not teaching, and not wearing the robes of the *gö-kar chang-lo'i dé* for ceremonial purposes, he wears traditional western dress. The traditions from which he chooses, however, range from an English gentleman's tweed, through sartorially elegant cowboy and Mississippi gambler attire, to Hassidic black. Everything is classical—but he mixes and matches amongst a range of previously unrelated cultures. The reason I mention this is because one's choice of teacher need not reflect the totally conventional suit: I am addressing the question of elegance, quality, verve, and timelessness—not conservatism. For elegance, quality, verve, and timelessness—read wisdom, compassion, energy, and the space in which they play. According to this principle, our choice of a teacher has to be based on increasing our skills of perception through practice. The less we understand of clothing, the more we need advice; the less we know of the realized state, the more we need to rely on applying the practice in order to develop our experience.

This leads naturally into the next stage. We have studied and practiced. We have developed our sense of how enlightened qualities are manifested. The next stage is finding a lama whom we appreciate intellectually, emotionally, and intuitively. We need to feel sympathetic and strongly drawn to move in that direction. We suspect at long last that this could be "home." We are ready for a relationship; whether this turns out to be the right one, we will need to discover. Next comes being with the lama and getting the encouraging feeling that maybe this time things really do stand a chance of evolving. Finally, from our experience of practice and transmission, we develop the unshakable confidence that things have evolved—and will definitely evolve further in the future. If we stay with this lama, at some point, in some lifetime, complete realization is inevitable.

At this point there is discontinuity—a jump. In spite of the gradual development of confidence, in the end there is always a leap of faith. The gradual process still brings us to the challenge of instantaneous immediacy. In Vajrayana there is no getting away from paradox. When the non-dual inseparability of form and emptiness is expressed in the language of logic, or from a linear perspective, the expression always turns out to be a paradox. No matter how great our confidence, there always remains the distance between the diving-board and the water. Our confidence in the lama can never be one hundred percent before we make vajra commitment, because one hundred percent confidence would actually mean complete realization. In the relative world of ordinary mind there is always some lingering doubt: Why does my lama enjoy spaghetti westerns? Did my lama just forget to answer my letter or does this mean something? Why does my lama keep telling the same joke over and over and laughing uproariously each time?

When the student is aware of having received ultimate benefit from the relationship, this leap into the space of commitment is made more glorious and exhilarating, easier but more breathtaking, devoid of concept but more meaningful. The more we have tried to be sensible and practical, to calculate and guarantee the benefits, the less exciting and the less significant the event, and the more unfinished business will loom up later in the relationship.

Because this is the theory, it expresses the form aspect of the relationship. But there is also the emptiness aspect, which can be inspirational and instantaneous—a moment's blinding understanding that everything we had ever hoped for could be found right here, like love at first sight. You might bump into a teacher on a remote hill path in India, exchange greetings without understanding a word of each other's language, have a cup of tea together, and ever after you would be able to acknowledge that the deal had been done there and then. This is not uncommon. But vajra relationship is not something to be swallowed unripe—it can only evolve organically from the place where one finds oneself. There needs to be some experience that is beyond spiritualized romanticism or esoteric wishful thinking. Danger arises only if we are in denial about this—denial of the uncertainty, vacillation, projection and dependency, fear of making choices, and self-imposed stress—our ordinary everyday moment-by-moment complicity with unenlightenment.

By definition, the terms of vajra relationship can only be set by those who confer it, not by those who request it. Ngak'chang Rinpoche describes it as follows:

> The heart of vajra commitment is simply being prepared to do anything. That preparedness is, in itself, a powerful catalyst of spiritual unfolding. This is something which reveals the portals on a vast, open dimension of relationship. It creates a sense of electricity in which the Lama is continually experienced as the doorway to an immense and unimaginable journey.[1]

This is an unusual but clearly recognizable state of mind. Chagdüd Tulku offers a view of a lama weighing up the situation with regard to his relationship with a body of his students:

> At the deepest level I recognised that the heart connection between a Lama and a real disciple had not yet ripened between me and any one of these monks. They respected and were devoted to me and thought me a worthy leader, but they were not yet ready to make their minds truly responsive to my guidance. I knew this because I myself had experienced the surrender of my self-willed direction to the guidance of my own lamas on many occasions. My lamas did not have to cajole me or convince me of the wisdom of their wishes. For example, when Tulku A-rig had told me to drop my worldly course of action and to practise, it was as though the powerful pulse of his pure heart had synchronised itself with my own heart's pulse. Nothing within me could possibly have contradicted him: I went straight into retreat.[2]

Milarépa said: "The day that I recognized my teacher as a Buddha, that was when I understood the nature of my own mind." There could hardly be a more succinct description of the pivotal moment of Vajrayana practice. Such simplicity is deeply stirring, but, in the moment of responding to Milarépa's words with enthusiasm, we begin to understand that what is being described is actually the realized state itself. Teacher and student are co-emergent in identical realization.

One Tantric model for realization is that bliss, the dynamism of form; and emptiness, the creative space of form; are described as co-emergent. In vajra relationship the teacher is always form, the actual presence of realization; while the student attempts to remain empty of agendas. The relationship bears fruit when the student receives authority to teach and to accept students in turn. Then the student, as a new teacher, practices with the experience of roles being reversed, and becomes accustomed to both aspects having the same flavor.

This is the characteristic taste of the lineage teachings themselves. They are lineage teachings—meaning not only teachings that are held by a lineage but teachings that are in essence about lineage—teachings that make lineage possible and actual, teachings of which lineage is the living expression. This is the physics by which the lineage coheres: the magnetism of lamas and the gravitation of students—a grand unified theory. In an overview of lineage, every lama is both a student-teacher and a teacher-student. The fringes of the teacher's mandala become epicenters of sibling mandalas of activity, portals for connections with new students. Lineage and mandala are thus non-dual, similar to the particle and wave theories of light. It would be foolish to suggest that the foundation for such a relationship should develop in any way other than gradually.

The Nyingma lama Dza Paltrül Rinpoche had a most extraordinary teacher, Do-khyentsé Yeshé Dorje, who was very much an heir of the mahasiddha tradition. Dza Paltrül himself appeared to be a simple, unpretentious, and humble person. His starting point was to lay out a most detailed description of the attributes one should look for in a teacher. While demurring that "nowadays it is difficult to find a teacher who has every one of the qualities described in the precious tantras,"[3] he insists that it is indispensable that a teacher should possess at least the following qualities: he or she needs to be pure; learned; well-versed in the scriptures; generous; pleasantly spoken; able to teach according to the individual; acting as he or she teaches; skillful at caring for disciples; matured by empowerments from an unbroken lineage; having kept the *samayas* (vows); being calm and disciplined, with few disturbing negative thoughts; having completely mastered Vajrayana practice—base, path, and result; having received visions of meditational deities; being liberated and realized; full of compassion; with few preoccupations; a passion for the Dharma; and repugnance for samsara.[4]

The great nineteenth century lama Jamgön Kongtrül Rinpoche not only describes the positive and negative qualities a student should look for in a master but also the converse: what the master should look for in a student. Each should avoid those who lack compassion; suffer anger, pride, and attachment; and who are undisciplined in word or deed.[5] In terms of the negative qualities of a student against which lamas should guard, Ngak'chang Rinpoche and Khandro Déchen commented to me as follows:

> Ourselves excepted—it is worthy of consideration to note that the Lama takes grave risks when accepting students into vajra relationship. Those who request vajra relationship with their Lama are almost always totally sure that they are sincere. They rarely question their own integrity or stability. Prospective vajra students often make the most extravagant assertions regarding their devotion, and feel insulted when they are asked to question themselves in even the smallest degree. Often everything is fine until the Lama asks a student to correct their antisocial or narcissistic behaviour—at which point the student suddenly loses their "devotion" and sets out on a campaign to demonise the Lama. We have seen such campaigns and have been deeply saddened by them. Some have amounted to no more than gossip-mongering, but some have been taken as far as articles and books wherein veracity has counted for no more than the authors' previous spu-

rious devotion. We have seen this happen to excellent Lamas of several lineages—and would say that hell hath no fury as a student who feels scorned.

Many of the great lineage Lamas who have come to the west, or who have taught western people, appear to throw all caution to the wind in terms of agreeing to work with the most unsavoury personalities our hemisphere has to offer. Their compassion has been so evidently unlimited that they have not protected themselves in any way—but rather have attempted to help even those with obvious psychological disorders. Antisocial personality disorders and narcissistic personality disorders are the most usual undercurrents beneath the disaffected western ex-students who launch invective at their erstwhile Lamas. We would therefore admonish all those who approach Lamas other than ourselves to take real responsibility, to act honourably, and to forswear idle promises built on temporary emotionalism.

The recommendation implicit in these teachings, that has been explicitly endorsed from the Buddha himself to the present day, and that also accords with the common sense of our own era, is that the student must take personal responsibility for investigating and validating the teacher. Ngakpa Rig'dzin Shikpo writes:

> Once a teacher has unequivocally been confirmed by a realised teacher of his own tradition, then it is up to the student to use his own judgement as to which of the confirmed teachers he feels particularly drawn and, if this connection is mutually felt, the student can feel reasonably confident in embarking on a pupil-teacher relationship. Failing this, he has to rely solely on his own judgement, possibly a hazardous undertaking . . .[6]

My own lamas, Ngak'chang Rinpoche and Khandro Déchen, have been unequivocally confirmed by Kyabjé Künzang Dorje Rinpoche

and Jomo Sam'phel, and by other lamas of the Nyingma tradition—
and I, in turn, have received their confirmation with regard to teaching those who approach me for help in following the Vajrayana.
Confidence stretches in two directions from this—the student has
confidence in the lama and the lama has confidence in his or her own
teacher's confirmation. Thus a confirmed teacher, especially one such
as myself, is a servant of the lineage. I try my best to honor this and not
to bring the lineage of my lamas into disrepute. And I expect my students to test me in the same way I tested my own lamas. Asvaghosa
discusses the importance of testing and knowing the lama:

> In order for the words of honour of neither the Guru nor the
> disciple to degenerate, there must be a mutual examination be-
> forehand (to determine if each can) brave a Guru-disciple rela-
> tionship.[7]

Asvaghosa says the vajra master should be an extremely stable person, with body, speech and mind completely under control. The
meaning of "stability" and "control" in this context refers to the stability of rigpa, and the "activity which is controlled through innate freedom." Mutual examination is stressed: not only must the student test
the lama, but the lama must test the student. The obligation of a
Vajrayana Buddhist is to investigate with care, intelligence, and maturity based on serious practice.[8]

But how can students assure themselves that their prospective
teacher possesses any of the appropriate qualities? The usual answer
is that the tradition of Vajrayana, in which every teacher in turn is
the disciple of another teacher in an unbroken line going back to the
beginnings of the lineage, can give the practitioner some security.
Having met several of my lama's vajra masters—particularly Kyabjé
Künzang Dorje Rinpoche and Jomo Sam'phel—this seems a self-
evident understanding. The recommendations of other lamas are reliable pointers that a student can follow, and, as such, I have had

the recommendation of Tharchin Rinpoche, Gyaltsen Rinpoche, Khenpo Sonam Tobgyal Rinpoche, Tulku Thubten Rinpoche, Chökyi Wangchuk Rinpoche, and several other lamas. These lamas have assured our Sangha that our teachers are authentic vajra masters. Khenpo Sonam Tobgyal demonstrated this in the most profound manner by attending Ngak'chang Rinpoche's teaching on *chod* (*gCod*) at Pema 'ö-Sel Ling[9] and receiving from him the empowerments of Tröma Nakmo and Machig Labdrön.[10]

Ngak'chang Rinpoche himself was advised by both His Holiness Düd'jom Rinpoche and His Holiness Dilgo Khyentsé Rinpoche to take Kyabjé Künzang Dorje Rinpoche as his vajra master. The highest lamas in a living lineage influence their influential disciples, who have disciples in turn, and so on. At the same time the fidelity of discipleship is always directly to one's immediate lama. So when all the disciples know how to remain empty to the lama's form—that which manifests is known as lineage.

But in the end it still comes down to personal responsibility, and the student's own experience of practice and transmission. These interlocking guarantees could be said to run the same risk as a piece of knitting. The whole depends on every part to retain its integrity, and if even one stitch is dropped, it can all quickly start to unravel. Ultimately, no one can take responsibility for the vows held by anyone else. Every stitch is dependent on every other stitch, and that which holds them together is devotion. But that too implies responsibility because every other stitch is dependent on oneself.

This means that ultimate responsibility is to be able to depend on oneself. It is incumbent upon the student to validate him or herself as a truthful, sincere, and straightforward student, through thorough self-examination at a higher level of honesty than is commonly expected in the "new age" marketplace. With that understanding, the entire edifice of lineage flickers between emptiness and form. This reveals how devotion is itself a primary practice of non-duality, hence Shakyamuni Buddha's remark that the end of the path is reached solely through devotion. Although devotion is the essence of the teacher-student relationship, what makes devotion possible is trusting oneself to keep one's vows, which in turn makes one a dependable focus for others.

Dza Paltrül said (and His Holiness Dala'i Lama constantly and emphatically echoes him) that before following a teacher, one first needs to examine that person. His Holiness Dala'i Lama has said that one could spend as many as thirteen years (a complete Tibetan calendar cycle, and an extra year in addition) studying the lama's teaching and testing the prospective vajra master. During this time the teacher acts in the capacity of spiritual friend—a mentor whose directives one is not bound to follow. By the end of this thirteen-year period, however, it is vital to have reached some definite conclusion about the teacher's ability in relation to oneself, and one's potential in relation to the teacher.[11]

I once met a Tibetan Buddhist practitioner from Greece, who told me a story about her first lama. She was in the first flush of utter dedication to practice, and she requested this lama to be her root teacher. But instead of accepting her right away, he gently invited her to tell him all about herself, about her life and her problems, and to take time for the two of them to get to know each other. He said she could take as long as thirteen years to do this; and after that, if she still so desired, he would give her an empowerment which would seal their relationship. But before the thirteen years were up, she had in fact settled down as the disciple of another teacher in a different school. For that very reason she remembers her first lama as having been her finest spiritual friend—and the one who paved the way for her discovery of her root teacher.

We need to contribute to clearing the ground ourselves through intensive practice. This is called ngöndro, the foundation practice that precedes the actual path. From this, an understanding is gained of what it actually would be like to work with this teacher in the context of vajra relationship. We need to feel understood, seen by the lama, so that our mind-states are transparent to the compassionate arc-light of the lama's gaze.

The Tantric foundation practice can be reflected in the teacher-student relationship itself: lamas are always stimulating, teasing, and challenging their students to be conscious of their tendency to prioritize or take refuge in passing mind-moments, the ever-changing contents of mind, as contrasted with the unchanging nature of Mind; to cycle between dualistic positions of "yes" and "no," "this" and "that" in their life-experience. This can be observed in their very relationship with the experience of the teacher.

Students need to develop some personal insight about their prospective teachers. For instance, they should have some sense of their lamas dissolving their experience of themselves into emptiness and re-emerging as the *yidam* (awareness-being, meditational deity) when giving an empowerment. They should ask themselves: what difference does this make to me? How does my experience of this change with practice? How is transmission experienced on all manner of other occasions, outside the formal window of opportunity provided by the empowerment—in the domain of the Dzogchen master? In addition, there is also "practicing the practice" of vajra commitment before actually taking any vows: regarding the lama as vajra master, and experimenting with living this view. Ngak'chang Rinpoche writes:

> You need the experience of having ignored advice, in terms of your life circumstances, and discovering your own "deeply convinced rationale" to be unreliable. You need the experience of having taken advice which you found very difficult and seeing the beneficial consequences quite acutely. Finally; you need to become totally bored, irritated, and frustrated with having your own rationale as the final deciding factor in everything that you do. You must come to see your rationale as a cage from which you are determined to escape; not because you cannot take responsibility for your life, but because you are expert at taking responsibility within the parametres of everyday life.[12]

A student once described the process she had gone through in trying to decide whether to stay in California or move to New York. She
made a list of the attractive and unattractive qualities of each place in
order to compare them. But somewhere in the process she began to
realize that all she was doing was trying to come up with pseudo-
rational reasons for making what was basically a purely arbitrary
choice—something her teacher had told her at the beginning of her
process. We do this all the time. What we like to think of as our freedom of choice is in fact the dubious freedom to conform to our own
neuroses and limited understanding, and to rationalize it after the fact
with pseudo-logic. No matter how much consideration we give, or
how many lists we make, there are some possibilities that will simply
never occur to us because they are outside the realm of what we consider to be our identities. We say: "I would never do/wear/say a thing
like that" (quite often without even being aware of it) and we thereby
constrain our "free" choice. We only do things with which our ego can
comfortably identify. But the suggestions of the vajra master, being
unconditioned, come to us from a different realm of being. After years
spent in the stale chamber of our own rationale, the input of the vajra
master can seem like the first breath of fresh air one has known in
quite some time. Khandro Déchen commented to me:

> There is actually nothing worse than having everything your
> own way. There would be nothing more claustrophobic than
> having a partner who agreed with you all the time, nothing more
> depressing than being able to design existence according to your
> own quality judgements. There is therefore nothing more use-
> less than having a Lama whose advice is conditional on your own
> agreement with it. The Lama is there to wreck our personal pat-
> terns of samsara in order that we can become vast in our appreci-
> ation rather than contracting and becoming more rigid. The
> Lama is always pointing at the beautiful scenery which lies out-
> side the safety of our comfortable cages.

...at this point vajra relationship begins to make intuitive sense. Once we perceive the small space of our habitual mind, we begin to long for the open vastness we have glimpsed in the eyes of the lama. We begin to understand that in giving up the dubious freedom of following our dualistic rationale, we are in fact losing nothing and gaining the possibility of everything. When one is accepted as the disciple of a vajra master, what actually occurs is that, out of their endless compassion, they agree to commit themselves utterly to our realization. They will never abandon us—not even if we abandon them and give up on ourselves. They remain as a constant manifestation of reality—*chö*, "as it is"—in our life that will always be there no matter how many years or even lifetimes we may take to understand or appreciate it.

There is nothing more significant that one human being can do for another.

3

THE HEART OF VAJRAYANA

The relationship with the vajra master is made not just for this life but is renewed in all future lives until enlightenment is attained. When enlightenment eventually dawns, the student will have become the equal of "all the enlightened ones of the past." Until then, the magnetism of this particular vajra master's transmission, the single key to that future, exceeds the inspiration even of the legends of other Buddhas.

When relationship with the teacher enters the Tantric phase, the lama becomes the path of practice in person. At this point it is no longer viable to judge the lama according to any criteria—even according to the criteria of the same vows one is attempting to keep oneself. This is true whether the lama is monastic, a non-monastic householder and parent, or a wisdom-eccentric apparently unconstrained by conventional behavior. Ngak'chang Rinpoche explained this to me in conversation:

If Vajrayana teachers are ordained according to the vows of the Sutras they may appear to their Vajrayana disciples as pure monks or nuns—or they may appear to contravene the vinaya (the monastic vows) in order to benefit their students. If Vajrayana teachers are ordained according to the vows of Tantra they may appear to their Vajrayana disciples as perfect *ngakpas* or *ngakmas*—or they may appear to contravene their samayas in order to benefit their students. If Vajrayana teachers are wisdom eccentrics, they may appear to their Vajrayana disciples as wonderfully outrageous examples of crazy wisdom, or they may appear as ordinary people without any special distinguishing signs—in order to benefit their students. One takes vajra commitment to avoid the slipperiness of one's own rationale. Therefore, all attempts to side-step the effectiveness of Vajrayana by calling the vajra master into question by any means whatsoever must be abandoned—or vajra relationship is non-functional. It is not that the vajra master is a person who cannot be questioned per se, but rather that the Vajrayana student needs to move beyond the trough of dualistic courtroom procedures in which they evade the lama through employing the lawyer of self-serving intellectual manipulation. This relationship is the living core of Vajrayana—and without it, Vajrayana becomes merely another methodology. Without the vajra master there is no Vajrayana.

Because of this, any form of judgment or critique applied to the vajra master after entry into vajra commitment cuts at the root of the relationship. By projecting inadequacies onto the vajra master one becomes oneself an obstacle to the flow of transmission. Instead, one attempts the practice of pure vision. Dza Paltrül Rinpoche describes it as follows:

However incomprehensibly the teacher may behave, always maintain pure perception, and recognize his way of doing things as his skillful methods.[1]

Pure vision means viewing the vajra master as continuously acting for the benefit of beings, and regarding all of his or her behavior as manifestations of unceasing enlightened activity.

At the level of Dzogchen, pure vision entails relating to the vajra master in terms of the three kayas: actively "taking the three kayas of the Lama as the path." This practice derives from the first three of the Fourteen Tantric Root Vows. The three kayas (spheres or 'bodies') are the dimensions of the Lama's realized existence: Mind (Tib. *chö-ku*, Skt. *dharmakaya*), energy (Tib. *long-ku*, Skt. *sambhogakaya*) and body (Tib. *trül-ku*, Skt. *nirmanakaya*). These relate, respectively, to the lama as follows: In the sphere of unconditioned potentiality (the womb of primal creativity, chö-ku or dharmakaya), the vajra master is presence display. Presence display signifies the presence of realization—a peripatetic hole in the fabric of our dualistic reality. One could enter this free space and make a connection at the level of the nature of Mind. In the sphere of intangible appearances (non-dual energy, long-ku or sambhogakaya) the vajra master manifests personality display. Personality display is the vividly colorful spontaneous expression of realization, beyond the possibility of dualistic conditioning—no matter how it manifests. In the sphere of realized manifestation (non-dual form, trül-ku or nirmanakaya) the vajra master manifests life-circumstances display. Life-circumstances display is the apparent obstacles, accidents, or suffering in the life of the vajra master, and also his or her fortunate circumstances. But, whatever occurs in this context, it is regarded as a manifestation of the vajra master's compassionate activity.

These three kayas are the vajra master's play of ability and effectiveness. This appears as the display of the presence of realization, as the display of phantom (empty) personality, and as the display of ephemeral life-circumstances. The *Tantrika* takes these three as the ultimate practice support, because their transmission is in itself the clarification of the practitioner's own mind, energy, and body. The vajra master represents the completion of the path in person.

There is a common misconception that enlightenment involves the personality being extinguished. All realized beings are expected to be bland smiling clones of each other, with any deviation from this seen as an unfortunate lapse from "perfection." At the level of emptiness, of course, all enlightened beings are the same, but at the level of form they are infinite in their variety. But emptiness and form are not separate. In the realized state, personality continues to exist but it is empty, impermanent, spontaneously compassionate, reflexive, responsive, communicative, and empathic. And this compassionate activity may take on infinite forms.

The practice of taking the three kayas of the lama as the path has no ritualized opening of windows of opportunity, no supporting sub-stratem of symbolism, no self-advertisement whatsoever. It is completely spontaneous, effortless, and direct, therefore only really accessible to students who either already have a profound relationship with the lama, an extraordinary karmic connection, or who are genuinely superior beings. The mahasiddha Kukkuripa said:

If conscious effort and striving are present, the Buddha is absent. Rituals and offerings are futile, but within the experience of the Lama's displays The Buddha is present. However; will the fortunate disciples see it?[2]

It is impossible to approach vajra relationship through mundane value judgements. The third Do-drupchen Rinpoche warned that true discrimination might run completely counter to common sense:

Among the false tertons there are many who are harmonious with people, who seem to have disciplined conduct, and are fortunate and charismatic. At the same time, among the authentic tertons there are many who are loose in speech and behavior and who, without the least hesitation, get involved in many activities that people will condemn. In that way the ter-tons take many grave obstructions of the doctrine on themselves in the form of infamy and ill repute and they use them for the practice of taking every experience in the great equal taste.[3]

Do-drüpchen Rinpoche therefore comments on the great yogis and yoginis:

One cannot judge tertons as inauthentic because of their imper-fect and mercurial character, even to the slightest extent.

And he continues by quoting Padmasambhava himself:

The hidden enlightened beings appear in uncertain form; the fool-deceivers are great hypocritical mimics of the dharmic prac-titioner. O people! Do not take gold and dross as equal.[4]

These are important statements for the student of Vajrayana. They represent the incontrovertible fact that the role of the vajra master cannot be adapted, which overturns every idea put forward by those who would attempt to legislate constraints and guidelines. Ngak'chang Rinpoche and Khandro Déchen wrote on this subject:

If those who lack realization form a committee which sets up standards to which their teachers must conform, then what could such teachers teach that such students could not teach them-selves—without the necessity of having a teacher? If the com-mittee is composed of realized beings, why should they dictate the behavior of other realized beings—when they understand that realized behavior is unbounded? If they do not understand that realized behavior is unbounded, then they are evidently not realized and therefore disqualified from making any comment on those who are.[5]

What should be most striking to the authentic Vajrayana student is that, out of all the teachers of all times, it is this particular lama who has manifested in the student's life right now. This is the lama whom the student has had the karmic fortune to meet. This is the ground for vajra commitment—the great unique contract for this life and beyond. The relationship with the vajra master is made not just for one life but is renewed in all future lives until enlightenment is attained. When enlightenment eventually dawns, the student will have become the equal of "all the enlightened ones of the past." Until then, the magnetism of this particular vajra master's transmission, the single key to that future, exceeds the inspiration even of the legends of other buddhas. The vajra master brings the student into his or her lineage of transmission. This lama is the gateway to relationship with all the buddhas. Without this present, living teacher, buddhas and buddhahood would remain merely objects of fantasy.

On the absolute level, the vajra master is unified with the very nature of our own mind, which is itself the essence of buddhahood. Through the outer vajra master and his or her teachings, we can come to the realization of the inner or absolute lama—which is the state of rigpa itself. If we could know the lama's innermost Mind, we would discover that the lama is equal in all aspects and qualities to a buddha. To have full confidence in him or her is therefore the only sure way to progress towards enlightenment.

The available literature devoted to this subject is quite extensive, even in translation. It dates from Padmasambhava and Yeshé Tsogyel to the present day, and it can be found in all the Tibetan schools. Some can probably be found on almost every Vajrayana practitioner's bookshelf. Jamgön Kongtrül, at the end of the nineteenth century, estimated that the authoritative texts on the subject must run into thousands. But one wonders how widely they are read, or understood, by people such as those western buddhists who would like to reduce the role of the vajra master, or eliminate it entirely. I once had an astounding conversation with a prominent western buddhist teacher who maintained that "surely, the terms of vajra commitment wer toriously undefined by scripture." Nothing could be further from the truth, as witness these definitive quotations. Padmasambhava said:

All the teachings and Tantras explain that at this present time when you have obtained the fortune of a human body after being on errant paths for innumerable æons, you should, free from the three spheres of concept, offer your body, life, and spouse to the master who shows the path of unexcelled enlightenment.

You should know that the master is more important than the Buddhas of a hundred thousand aeons. Because all the Buddhas of the æons appeared through following masters. There will never be any Buddhas who have not followed a master. The master is the Buddha, the master is the Dharma, likewise the master is also the Sangha. He is the embodiment of all the Buddhas. He is the nature of Vajradhara. He is the root of the Three Jewels. Keep the command of your vajra master without breaking even a fraction of his words. If you break the command of your vajra master you will fall into the unceasing Vajra Hell from which there will be no chance for liberation. By serving your master you will receive the blessings. Do not regard the master and the yidam as different, because it is the master who introduces the yidam deity to you. By always venerating the master at the crown of your head you will be blessed and your obstacles will be cleared away.[6]

His Holiness Dilgo Khyentsé Rinpoche writes:

It is said that all the Buddhas of the three times . . . achieve Buddhahood through reliance on a spiritual teacher. The essence of reliance on a teacher is unceasing devotion . . . It protects our practice from obstacles and ensures progress on the path. Devotion to the teacher is thus the core of all our spiritual practice, regardless of the particular stages of the path we cultivate . . . Although the guru at first may appear to us in ordinary human form and although he may at first appear to behave in an ordinary human way, his mind really is inseparable in nature from the Mind of the Buddha. The qualities of the guru differ in no way from those of a perfectly enlightened Buddha . . . Actually, the only difference between the guru and the Buddhas is that his kindness exceeds that of all the enlightened ones of the past.[7]

Asvaghosa writes:

A disciple with the good qualities of compassion, generosity, moral self-control, and patience should never regard as different his Guru and the Buddha Vajradhara.[8]

He stresses the importance of making offerings to the lama, and says one should never even stand in the guru's shadow, step over their shoes or sit in their seat. This degree of reverence may seem extreme to modern day westerners, but it should be understood as method—a way of remaining in an alert and receptive state in the presence of the lama, through attentiveness to him or her at every level. We view the lama's life as more important than our own and we practice taking care of them, anticipating their every need and wish, and working to manifest their vision.

Different lamas will accept different degrees of formality in terms of how such methods of devotion are applied. Some will allow the ambience suggested by Asvaghosa, while some will abjure such tokens of reverence. But whatever mode operates, the method is chosen in order to be of the greatest benefit to a particular sangha. Some students who have been used to a reverential environment have been shocked by the informality of Ngak'chang Rinpoche and Khandro Déchen. Conversely, some who are new to the teachings of Vajrayana are surprised at my teachers' complete unwillingness to enter into dispute or debate with them. To those who know Ngak'chang Rinpoche and Khandro Déchen well, it becomes evident that the respect offered comes in terms of willingness to listen. Ngak'chang Rinpoche commented on this to me when I first began to teach:

> The most important factor for a student, in being a student, is that they develop a sense of openness. This does not mean blind acceptance of whatever the lama says. It simply means acknowledging the lama as one who may well have a more interesting way of looking at things. One is only a student because one wishes to change. If one has no desire to change—why would one seek a teacher? If all one wishes is information, then it is better found in books. The principle of respect for the teacher should be based on openness to the possibility of being confused. To be a student, one has to have some knowledge of the fact that one's logic is shot through with dualistic errors of all kinds—and that it is therefore worth presenting the lama with one's confusion and incomprehension in the expectation of its being resolved.

Whether or not we achieve realization depends entirely upon our devotion to the lama. If disciples possess the "ring" of faith and devotion, then the "hook" of the vajra master's wisdom and compassion will pull them swiftly to liberation. In Tibet, the tradition seeped into the air of the remotest canyon out of the very rocks of the landscape. Buddhist practitioners in the Himalayas, as any visitor there has discovered, take inspiration with complete naturalness from countless details of everyday existence. There has never been such a person in the Tibetan tradition as a tantrika without a lineage, or without a lama.

His Eminence Kalu Rinpoche said:

> Once we have . . . accepted that person as our Vajrayana teacher, the only attitude that is appropriate is one of complete confidence

in that teacher. Whether that teacher is enlightened or not, we should consider that teacher as an enlightened Buddha. If we develop negative attitudes . . . then we have committed the first [i.e. greatest] root downfall of the Vajrayana.[9]

Khandro Déchen elucidated further on this subject in conversation:

It is not a question of whether the vajra master is enlightened or not. The principle is that the effectiveness of regarding the vajra master as enlightened is independent of the actual status of the Lama. How could I act as a vajra master unless this were true? There have even been cases where disciples have gained realisation through practising with fraudulent teachers—which is an indication of the colossal power of devotion within vajra relationship. Through working within the structure of Vajrayana and maintaining its precepts, both Lama and disciple manifest the lineage of Padmasambhava and Yeshé Tsogyel. Without this, the lineages of Vajrayana have no future.

Asvaghosa discusses the dangers of becoming the disciple of a lama and subsequently indulging in one's own rationale to the extent that one comes to despise that lama. He states:

Having become the disciple of such a protecting [guru], should you despise him from the heart, you will reap continual suffering as if you had disparaged all the Buddhas.[10]

Sufferings that may be incurred traditionally include disease, death by poisonous snakes, and boiling in hell. The six realms of existence as physical locations is a view inherited from ancient Indian culture. In Buddhism, the inner meaning relates to the perceptual anguish of the various deluded samsaric mind states. So although one need not fear the actuality of snake bites as a result of disparaging one's lama, the psychological consequences are no less significant to one's spiritual health.[11]

Our perception can certainly become poisoned by narcissism, and the result of indulgence in such a self-centered rationale can certainly lead to hellish mind states in which one tortures oneself with one's own self-aggrandizing concepts. To be unable to trust and have confidence in a lama who has shown us nothing but kindness, who exhibits endless patience and energy in helping others, and who has invested significant time and effort in our spiritual welfare, is clearly an unfortunate psychological state. To regard something as valuable and important, to take the major step of committing oneself to a teacher, and then to come to despise that teacher is its own unique form of personal psychological hell. If we continue to prioritize our narcissism, we may start to see negative motivation in the lama's actions, and begin judging everything about the lama by the unreliable, dualistic yardstick of our deluded rationale. Our whole experience of the relationship will become diseased, poisoned, and hellish if we view it through the lens of our own self-interest.

We will also do severe damage to ourselves as practitioners—not only of Vajrayana but of any spiritual path. It would be extremely difficult ever again to trust anything apart from our own self-serving perception, and therefore difficult or impossible to make any kind of wholehearted commitment to a teacher or practice in the future. Once we have gone back on our vows, it would be extremely difficult to be able ever to take them again with the same sincerity and enthusiasm. It would require a dramatic shift in perception—and this shift would be as great or greater than the shift we were unable to make that caused the breakage of vows in the first place. Vajrayana practice is not possible without vajra commitment, and so one would lose access to Vajrayana completely. It is for this reason that the prospective Vajrayana student should spend as long as necessary, up to the traditional thirteen years, experimenting with vajra relationship before taking vows and becoming a disciple. A hasty decision which one later came to regret would be disastrous. Once vajra commitment has been taken, regret cannot be entertained.

Nevertheless, it is vital to understand that this commitment must be based on real experience. One needs to know, at the most fundamental level, that this lama can guide one to realization. This sense of knowing may flicker as a result of one's neurotic personality, but if there has been real experience of transmission, that experience will remain, at least in memory. A Vajrayana student can always return to that memory as a source of inspiration. This is absolutely necessary if one is to continually view the vajra master's activities with pure vision. It is the basis of lama'i naljor or guru yoga—the act of continually re-entering the dimension of the lama's transmission. Through lama'i naljor one re-enacts the experience of empowerment one has received, thereby strengthening one's commitment and the fire of one's devotion.

The amazing quality of Vajrayana is that pure vision can be effective regardless of the actual qualities of the teacher. Pure vision is a method that appears to be directed outward, but which actually has its greatest effect on the mind of the practitioner. There is the well-known story of the dog's tooth that was venerated by an old lady as the tooth of the Buddha until the strength of her devotion invested it with miraculous powers. Similarly, there are famous stories of students who achieved realization in dependence upon teachers who did not have any themselves.

If a student really had the degree of development to be able to understand the practice so incisively, he or she could relate to the teacher's inherent realization, even if it had not been stabilized in practice. This is actually feasible. The method of vajra relationship is lama'i naljor, which is the essential practice of Vajrayana, in both Tantra and Dzogchen.

In Tantra we visualize the lama as an awareness-being (yidam) and merge with him or her in that form. Viewing the lama as an awareness-being helps us overcome any deluded tendency we might have to see faults and shortcomings in our teacher. Only practitioners with very great devotion are able to practice lama'i naljor using the image of their own flesh-and-blood teachers.

One would require the lama's permission to attempt that, and historically only certain extremely eminent lineage holders have ever acceded to such a request. The atmosphere of devotion and pure perception around those lamas had extended so widely through not just their lineage but their entire school and beyond, that the "certain audience" for the practice had been resoundingly constituted. Visualizing the lama in a symbolic form makes it easier to generalize the sense of guru yoga, so as to embrace all of one's teachers in this life: Buddhist and non-Buddhist, spiritual and worldly, educational and familial. When the lama appears in a symbolic energized context, the extraordinary visionary image of a meditation-being, one is easily inspired to view all those persons as having accumulated into this magnificent display. But to appreciate them as inseparable from the ordinary human form of the teacher is usually considered more difficult for the average student. Without enormous devotion, there would be a risk of subtly perverting the practice, accommodating it to one's limitations. One might find oneself projecting some cycle of roles onto the lama: parent projection, partner projection, lover projection, buddy projection, colleague projection, boss projection, monarch projection, professor projection . . . Practicing like that might seem to have a face value that flatters the teacher, but the practice would actually be devaluing itself through inflation. One would be subverting the status of the teacher by classifying it into a repertoire of personnae acknowledged by the ordinary mind. One might lose the vital perception of the ordinary nirmanakaya of the teacher as inseparable from the dimensions of mind and energy that are the source of the teacher's transmission: the extraordinary in the apparently ordinary, the essentially extraordinary in the superficially extraordinary, the fundamentally ordinary in the essentially extraordinary.

If one does attain this level of devotion, however, it catalyzes one's practice to an unprecedented degree. It enables the lamas to manifest even greater effectiveness, because they can then function to the full extent of their capabilities. It is said that if we just visualize our vajra masters with clarity and vividness—even for an instant—this is of greater benefit than meditating upon a hundred thousand other yidams. The Kadampa teacher Gyalsé Ngülchu Thogmé had no practice other than meditating on his lama and serving him with body, speech, and mind his whole life. Ngak'chang Rinpoche, in a private letter to me, said of his own tsa-wa'i lamas:

> Kyabjé Künzang Dorje Rinpoche and Jomo Sam'phel are such a vast radiance for me—both in my practice and my everyday life—that merely to think of them brings a smile to my face. I say this not as some kind of mealy-mouthed sycophant, or as a parrot of hollow sanctimonious rhetoric—but as a statement of raw directness. The actualisation of the realised state itself would be meaningless without Kyabjé Künzang Dorje Rinpoche and Jomo Sam'phel as its immaculate ornaments. This is not because I worship them or conceive of them as super-human—but because of the nature of the vows themselves, and how my teachers magnify the nature of those vows through their presence display, personality display, and life-circumstances display.
>
> Acting in any way to serve them enlivens my experience of life and galvanizes my practice. I can only say that it is my strongest wish that all Vajrayana practitioners come to recognize the qualities of the vajra master—and that their minds will not be poisoned by the rhetoric of those who are able to take refuge only in themselves.

Devotion to the lama and the lineage is the high-octane fuel in the engine of practice. Devotion is an unfashionable word in some quarters, so it may be worth considering its function. One way it arises is from trying to view oneself as the heir of one's teachers and the entire body of the lineage. This is so impossibly awesome to contemplate that the only way to accommodate it is by allowing the imaginary vessel of one's limited self-image to be shattered. This is something that western people can understand quite well from our familiarity with the experience of romantic love, which has been idealized in our culture for centuries. People in love describe their experience in the same way: "This thing is bigger than both of us." There is an ongoing fission-explosion of the sense of identity. One can no longer maintain the view of the self as "a container with its contents." This is not only a direct introduction to the experience of emptiness, even beyond that, it is an opportunity to experience emptiness as non-dual with the intensity of arising form as the manifestation of strong emotions.

Devotion is a shortcut to the hyper-space of realization. At its extreme, the effect of devotion is neither destructive nor creative, neither pleasurable nor painful, blissful nor agonizing. In moments of such intensity one can no longer say if the emotion is inside oneself or if one is inside the emotion. One could be standing, perhaps momentarily puzzled, at the threshold of non-dual experience—"neither this nor that, nor both, nor neither." Buddhism defines realization by rejecting the grand culturally dominant metaphors that derive from intellect alone: as oneness (monism); as something separate from oneself (dualism); as meaninglessness (nihilism); or as bestowing universal meaning (eternalism). But the acid-test of vajra relationship is that there is experience of transmission of the nature of Mind. This brings a sense of certainty that clearly does not arise through will or emotion, but which becomes the basis for a devoted relationship that is characterized by dedicated willpower and positive emotion. But those relative characteristics in and of themselves do not form the basis of the relationship. The whole discussion collapses if this essential point is not understood.

Devotion arises from trust: trust at a very deep level; trust in the lineage of the lama; trust in the commitment, dedication, and realization of the lama. The personality display of the lama may be very different from conventional views of behavior. The lama may act in what appears to be unusual or even outrageous ways. But with de-votion, the disciple puts up no barriers, and is able to be open and receptive to the transmission that can come through extremely diverse situations.

The life circumstances display of the lama may be chaotic, unortho-dox, or unpredictable from a conventional viewpoint, but it can be a source of inspiration when viewed as the lama's *kyil-khor* (*mandala*). The lives of the non-celibate teachers in particular are full of incidents of extraordinary behavior towards their disciples, but these incidents are recorded precisely because those circumstances gave rise to pro-found and significant results in the mind stream of the practitioners. No vajra master employs unusual methods without certainty that the results will be unusually positive. But this can only be judged in the long term, in the same way that certain medical treatments can only be gauged over a course of years.

Devotion means complete trust in the lama's desire for the disciple's realization of rigpa. Authentic devotion is empowering, because it frees us from confusion and doubt. If we have enough trust, we can allow ourselves to loosen our death-grip on our own rationale a bit. In the resulting chaos of unfamiliar emptiness we can rest in the form of the vajra master because it is unconditioned form—ceaseless compas-sionate activity.

Vajra relationship is not about abdicating responsibility for deci-sions in our lives; rather it concerns remaining always open to the ac-tivities and indications of the lama, and the directions in which these may take us. Transmission can occur through a look, a gesture, the lacerating shrapnel blast of raw horseradish when you were expecting the stodgy reassurance of mashed potatoes, some seemingly whimsical comment from one's teacher—anything. The more we can let go of our cramped habitual concepts about ourselves and our world, the more we can become accessible to the possibility of transmission in every moment.

Devotion is the ground that makes vajra relationship possible.

Without devotion there can be no vajra relationship, because vajra commitment requires letting go of one's rationale and entering a relationship of complete reliance on the enlightened nature of the vajra master. If we have confidence in the lama—if we have developed devotion—we will find "vajra commands" (or "vajra suggestions" as Ngak'chang Rinpoche and Khandro Déchen define their own approach to guidance) easy to accept. If we doubt the lama and place our confidence in our own subjectivity, we will find it difficult or impossible to appreciate challenges to our cherished habitual patterns and beliefs. This dependence on our own dualistic rationale holds us back from any form of Tantric practice, let alone the possibility of realization. But without firsthand experience of transmission and empowerment from a lama, devotion is difficult to understand.

According to Vajrayana theory, during an empowerment (Tib. *wang*, Skt. *abhisheka*) the lama is able to dissolve his or her experience of self into emptiness. That is to say, the lama becomes unconditioned by having an ordinary body, personality, and mind; then arises as the manifestation of the yidam or meditational deity, with the experience of embodying that in themselves. So, empowerment into the practice of a yidam is therefore conferred, in effect, by the yidam. The yidam is the energetic form of the Mind of a buddha and the empowering lama by direct inference is—a buddha. Unless one views the lama as a buddha, it is not possible to receive empowerment. It is this understanding which is the foundation for vajra relationship, and those who find themselves philosophically opposed to it in any way render themselves unable to approach Vajrayana.

Ngawang Thubten Nyima said:

You should prepare yourself for a wang as if you were going to receive consecration from the Buddha himself—as, in a sense, you are. During the preparation ritual performed by the Lama before the wang, he has created himself as the deity; throughout the wang you should think of the Lama as not different from the

deity, and visualise him in the form of the deity . . . The consecration is most effective if you cultivate a firm belief that you are
receiving the wang from the deity itself . . . If you understand
what you have received during the wang then you will feel a natural inclination to make vast offerings to the Lama out of recognition of his great kindness.[12]

Trungpa Rinpoche explained the origin of the Tantric method of
transmission as follows:

The ceremony of abhisheka is actually based on the example of
the Buddha. The Buddha appeared to [King Indrabhuti] in royal
costume and taught the first Tantra, the Guhyasamaja. That was
the first presentation of Tantra.[13]

The implication of this is deep and crucial. According to Tibetan
tradition, the formula for the relationship with the lama changes rad-
ically at the point of requesting transmission. Once we begin to engage
with Tantric empowerments, we have entered the world of the dangerous friend, the lama-disciple relationship. One is supposed to have
finished testing and experimenting long before, during the thirteen-
year period of evaluation. At this point, the only allowable action is
the leap over. Hence Dza Paltrül Rinpoche insists that, after receiving
empowerment:

You should never cease to consider [the teacher] to be the Buddha
in person . . . Each of his acts is simply the activity of a realised
being attuned to the nature of those he has to benefit . . . Always
act according to the teacher's wishes in every situation . . . like a
bridge, there should be nothing that we cannot bear, however
pleasant or unpleasant the tasks he asks us to do . . . The disciple
should be like a tsa-tsa[14] from the mould of the teacher.[15]

Pure vision means viewing the lama as a buddha and taking the three kayas of the lama as the path of practice. If a would-be Tantric student does not see the teacher as a buddha, this is called the first and greatest of the Fourteen Root Downfalls. It implies that the student has judged the teacher by the standards of ordinary morality and conventional concepts of how a spiritual personality should manifest. If neither student nor lama sees the other with pure vision, then that would imply a simple Sutric spiritual friendship or just an ordinary human relationship.

According to Vajrayana tradition, all practitioners who have taken empowerment from a lama are thereby in vajra relationship with that lama and with each other. Consequently they are supposed to be exercising these practices of pure vision. But this is not so easy in the context of public Tantric transmissions as given in modern times. Most audiences include a proportion of people who are simply not expecting to hear, not prepared to keep, or not in a position to keep, such commitments. So, nowadays, few lamas give any samayas (commitments to practice) along with a public empowerment. To quote Tsélé Natsok Rangdröl Rinpoche:

Some people claim that empowerments given to a crowd . . . are not the complete four empowerments of Secret Mantra, and that no fault exists since these are just permission-blessings or entrustments. But actually even an entrustment involves the samaya commitment to keep the deity in mind and do the practices of approach and accomplishment [generation and completion] and so forth. During such a ceremony one has to repeat the taking of the precepts of refuge, bodhicitta, and the samayas of the five families, and since most ordinary people cannot possibly know the principles of what should be adopted and avoided, both myself and others are therefore indeed at fault for being involved in such affairs. Incidentally, as it has been taught in the Sutras that people who live off selling the sacred dharma are reborn in a hell where they eat flaming iron balls and drink molten lead, it seems as though the dharma practitioners of the present age have incredibly great courage.[16]

Kyabjé Chhi-'mèd Rig'dzin Rinpoche once told a story about a conversation he had had with some other high Nyingma lamas. He stated that it was his intention to stop giving empowerments, because nobody ever kept the samayas he gave (though in my experience these have always been of the most minimal degree, such as to recite the mantra only seven times a day). His group of peers were shocked. How could you think of such a thing, they asked, your transmission line is very important, of course you mustn't stop giving empowerments. In that case, Kyabjé Chhi-'mèd Rig'dzin Rinpoche told them, he would continue to give empowerments, but he would give no samayas with them at all. It would be better, he said, if he suffered the karmic consequences of giving no samayas than if all these other people suffered the consequences of breaking them.

Obstacles are said to accrue to both lamas and students as a result of the disregard or bewilderment with which students sometimes treat these samayas. The students often suffer wrackings of conscience in trying to square new commitments with the ones they have already taken on from other lamas. For this reason, one of the first things that a teacher has to do in the west, when accepting a student's transition to discipleship, is to take karmic responsibility for sorting out and pruning the student's collection of incomprehensible commitments. The pure motivation of the student in requesting and following the lama's advice satisfies all samayas simultaneously. This means, therefore, that only the lama bears karmic responsibility for any problem that this advice may have created for the student.

A point that seems worth re-emphasizing is that the terms of vajra relationship do not define the role of the vajra master, which is understood to be beyond definition. The terms only define the role of the student, and far more stringently than in Sutra. In the Sutric tradition, the teacher/student relationship can always be checked against written rules and principles, and the Buddha made it clear before he died that these could be altered after his passing according to the requirements of time, place, custom, and individuals. But in Vajrayana, the emphasis is on an inner commitment, not an outer one: one uses one's awareness of the teacher from moment to moment.

The vow of pure vision is technically impossible to keep perfectly unless one is enlightened. How else could it be possible to see the teacher continuously as a buddha? As the proverb goes, when sentient beings look at buddhas they see sentient beings; when buddhas look at sentient beings they see buddhas. It could be said that the practice of pure vision falls into the category of experiences that are simply too advanced for most people. But at the same time it is also highly pragmatic, a self-fulfilling prophecy. As is common in spiritual practice, we begin with a game of "let's pretend," the ngöndro of "practicing the practice."

It is like learning any other kind of activity, playing a sport, for instance. To begin with, one is only imitating the moves, going through the motions. Eventually this develops the capacity to get closer and closer to the real thing. Then finally the day dawns when one is actually doing it, taking part in the great game itself. The more one tries to view other beings as buddhas, the more it becomes possible that one might have the actual experience of seeing them as buddhas. And the more one is viewed as a buddha oneself, the more it is supposed to confer the empowerment to behave with wisdom and compassion. As Trungpa Rinpoche put it: "ego wilts under the weight of its coronation robes."[17]

In their efforts to establish a true appreciation of the value of the vajra master as the heart of Vajrayana in the west, Ngak'chang Rinpoche and Khandro Déchen have addressed their own situation as vajra masters according to criteria that cut through the mentality that finds fault in any paradigm that affronts "political correctness." In a personal communication to their Vajrayana disciples, they commented:

Our approach to the vajra master rôle, in terms of how we function for our students in that position, is that being vajra masters is our practice. It is not simply what we are, on the basis of realization. That is only possible for those with realisation. For authentic vajra masters, those who actually embody the enlightened state, there is benefit in whatever they do—but for us, it has to be a matter of the most extraordinary responsibility. What is crucial, in terms of the realistic functioning of Vajrayana, is that the method of relating with the vajra master is fully functional whatever the realisation of the particular Lama. We say this because there are those in the west who seek to discredit the rôle of vajra master and thereby neuter the Vajrayana. In our effort to defend the Vajrayana and the rôle of vajra master, we feel we need to demonstrate this principle without allowing "the unprincipled" to take advantage of the example of our manifesting the vajra master role for those who authentically wish to practice Vajrayana.

The reason I feel at liberty to reveal this seemingly shocking assertion by my own lamas is that I have never met, and somehow think I never shall meet, a Buddhist teacher who claims to have reached the end of the path of practice. Whatever others may say about them, lamas always refer to themselves as practitioners. This, however, should not be understood as a statement proclaiming that "we're all in this together as more-or-less equals"—teachers and students all with their own practices. To take this view would be to fall into the slough of confusion that characterizes the woolly-minded liberal's dreary attempts to democratize the Vajrayana. Those who are afraid of anything which looks too effective in demolishing duality are always at pains to seize on statements of humility on the part of great lamas to validate their pallid philosophy of universal suffrage with regard to realization. Ngak'chang Rinpoche and Khandro Déchen's statement needs to be seen in the light of the situation which has developed in the western world. The confusion caused by those who wish to promote their independence from the authentic lineages needs to be addressed if the Vajrayana is to be preserved for future generations in the west. By pointing to this principle in a manner that allows no accusations of personal advantage, they are able to dismiss the specious clichés of contrived egalitarianism.

4

A TIME OF TRANSITION

The seductive ideal of freedom of choice is the dominant myth of our society, encouraging people to remain essentially adolescent up until retirement age or even death . . . It's more important to follow your feelings than to actually arrive at any particular goal. We have become more interested in process than result.

Over the last century, the tide of Vajrayana transmission has crossed the enormous geographical and psychological ocean from the east to the west. But it appears that there are some mismatches between traditional Vajrayana and current western cultural norms. We often fail to realize how much we are affected by the conceptual assumptions and psychological style of our native culture, because these appear as part of the neutral background of what we assume to be reality. However, western ideals of democratic egalitarianism and liberal humanism are fundamentally at odds with the Vajrayana, in theory and in practice. Some crucial messages of our Judeo-Christian heritage, such as the story of Adam and Eve being evicted from Paradise for eating from the Tree of Knowledge, make no sense in a Buddhist context. In addition, many of the particular qualities of common western neuroses such as depression, dependency, and eternal adolescence, present obstacles to forming a healthy relationship to the vajra master. We are all greatly affected by this, and our only defense against it is awareness.

We live in an age of quite unprecedented access to Buddhist culture: on the internet; in books; from world-traveling teachers; in databases; in every language, ancient and modern; from every angle of interpretation, application, and critique. A vast panoply of Buddhist teachings from a wide variety of cultures, all periods of history, and all phases of development can be summoned up instantaneously almost everywhere. This is certainly supportive to study, which may account for the continuing growth in popularity of "Buddhism of the intellect." From the Dzogchen perspective, however, this would be classified as Sutra.

It is probably no coincidence that Sutra rather than Tantra is what is usually practiced in the west, even when Sutra is presented to look somewhat like Vajrayana. The Sutric relationship with the lama is a method of study that superficially seems to harmonize with the liberal humanist values of many of the educated intellectual westerners who develop an interest in Buddhism. It is a style of practice in which the autonomy of the student is believed to be safeguarded. Ultimately, this can only reveal itself to be a paradox, because the peak of the Sutric path is the experience of emptiness—and in that experience one discovers that this "autonomy" is also empty of definable existence. The Buddhist/humanist parallel lines converge at that point.

Contrary to our cultural concepts, the liberal humanist is actually the victim of blind faith—faith that human reason is the ultimate cognitive tool in the universe. Any disciple of any lama in any Vajrayana lineage with sufficient experience of meditation practice knows otherwise. This is not well understood among western buddhists because for the most part we would prefer not to believe it. It somehow offends our egalitarian sensibilities to think that people could have different capacities in terms of understanding and experience, because we confuse this with a difference in absolute worth. But the Buddhist idea is that we are all beginninglessly enlightened, and the wide variety of teachings exist for the wide variety of students with their wide variety of confusion and delusion.

It is useful to return to an understanding of how the fabric of Tantric practice functions, in order to expose the flimsy synthetics with which some western buddhists would like to replace it. The main point is that Tantra goes beyond the rational intellect. Any attempt to describe non-duality through linear logic ends up in para-dox. Paradox is a display of words (such as "the gateless gate") that is employed to indicate enlightened experience. But this does not mean mere intellectual pyrotechnics: we engage with these fireworks senso-rially, sensually, and in the dimension of concept consciousness as one of the senses.[1] What is being conveyed can really only be understood by experiencing it as a transmission of the state, whether it is being blatantly described, whimsically finger painted, or indicated with a wordless gesture. To grasp at it with ordinary mind expresses one's intrigue and rapacity, irritation and discomposure, or disbelief and bemusement. Whether through attraction, aversion, or indifference, the intellect that tries to separate emptiness and form is caught be-tween the jaws of a dilemma of comprehension. The high-tension, unmediated, open space of Tantric transmission can never be ade-quately replaced by cool, leisurely, reflective "downloading," or any equivalent cerebral pastime.[2]

As we have shown, the essence of Tantric practice is relationship with the vajra master. To attempt the practice of Vajrayana without a commitment to a lama is not only unknown in history but appar-ently unworthy even of mention in the Vajrayana teachings. The Five Certainties—*ngé-pa nga* (*nges pa lNga*)—are held to be necessary in order to make Tantric transmission possible: the certain teacher (lama, vajra master)—*Tonpa* (*sTon pa*); the certain teaching (Va-jrayana/transmission of explanation)—*tenpa* (*bsTan pa*); the certain retinue (mandala of disciples)—*'khor* ('khor); the certain setting (place)—*né* (*gNas*); and the certain juncture (time)—*dü* (*dus*). Never-theless in the west today it is common to find practitioners uncertain of who is actually their lama or whether they belong to any particular lineage. They struggle through the Tantric foundation practices: making prostrations to the uncertain guru, making offerings to the uncertain guru, unifying with the mind of the uncertain guru, etc. Very worthy practitioners often blame their own lack of discipline if their interest in a formal repetitive practice inexplicably runs out of steam. Lack of discipline could occasionally be viewed as the form aspect of the problem, but the emptiness aspect is probably much more relevant, namely, lack of devotion.

Trungpa Rinpoche characterizes some problems in the west as stemming from misplaced generosity:

According to tradition, the teacher . . . should require that his students practise properly, in accordance with the tradition of the lineage. There are problems when a teacher is too kind to students who do not belong to the teacher's race and upbringing. Some teachers from the East seem to be excited by foreignness: "Wow! Finally we are going to teach the aliens, the overseas people." Because of this fascination and out of a naïve generosity, they make unnecessary concessions. Although such teachers may be liberal enough to include Western students, to take them to heart and be very kind to them, their extraordinary kindness may be destructive.[3]

Both in the west and also nowadays in the east it has become customary for lamas to perform certain empowerments somewhat in the manner of a blessing, an auspicious connection with the lama, lineage, and practice. Some high lamas, however, compromise by deliberately omitting to give out the critical details of how to perform the actual practice. They leave that to be transmitted by the personal teachers of those who are authentically practicing, at a time when they are best able to make use of the practice; such that the mantra, the sacred sound; and the envisionment, sacred luminosity, arrive fresh in the mind stream of a person who is appropriately prepared.

It seems that at some point in Tibetan history there began to be a shift away from the conditions in which classic Vajrayana empowerments had been given. Originally, the most important condition was that the Sutric phase of the relationship with the lama should definitely have borne some fruit. Trungpa Rinpoche described the transition as follows:

Traditionally, in medieval India and Tibet, the date for an abhisheka [wang, empowerment] was set six months in advance. In that way students would have six months to prepare. Later the Tantric tradition became extremely available, and some of the teachers in Tibet dropped that six-month rule—which seems to have been a big mistake. If we do not have enough time to prepare ourselves for an abhisheka, then the message doesn't come across. There is no real experience... The number of people who are going to receive a particular abhisheka is also very important ... the psychology that happens between the people involved and the environment that such people create are right at the heart of the matter ... Receiving hundreds and hundreds of abhishekas and constantly collecting blessing after blessing as some kind of self-confirmation has at times become a fad ... This was true in Tibet in the nineteenth century as well as more recently in the West. That attitude, which reflects the recent corruption in the presentation of Vajrayana, has created an enormous misunderstanding. People who collect successive abhishekas in this manner regard them purely as a source of identity and as a further reference point. They collect abhishekas out of a need for security, which is a big problem ...[4]

Trungpa Rinpoche's view was that, for cultural reasons, we cannot help but bring to Buddhism a certain style of, to use his now legendary expression, spiritual materialism. The implication is that we are not prepared to be satisfied merely with enlightenment. We want enlightenment, and we also want to be able to hear the applause as we gain it. Something in us quite likes the idea of processing slowly toward our Lion Throne as though receiving an Oscar, passing through an avenue formed by everyone we've ever known, glimpsing a tear of admiration in every eye, especially that of anyone who was maybe a bit sharp with us when we were adolescent . . . This ought to demonstrate quite vividly the Tantric view that unenlightenment is our own activity, something in which we all but continuously engage. This implies that we have an ambivalent relationship with enlightenment: it is something that we both want and do not want. We are not quite sure if we could sacrifice our dualistic personality, which would like both to have its cake and eat it.

Ngak'chang Rinpoche and Khandro Déchen have observed that it seems as though westerners possess an "extra layer of samsara" due to the fertile ground for neurosis that can be created by a nuclear (as opposed to extended) or fragmented family upbringing. The seductive ideal of freedom of choice is the dominant myth of our society, encouraging people to remain essentially adolescent up until retirement age or even death. Commitment to any one particular path is seen as narrowing one's options rather than focusing one's energy. It's more important to "follow your feelings" than to actually arrive at any particular goal. We have become more interested in process than result.

If that modus operandi were applied to the Buddhist path, results would arrive very quickly. But the Buddhist practitioner is wary of the temptation to polarize any given paradox into its extremes: as here, the possibility of separating the path and its result. But they are inseparable; so, any effort to dwell in them in isolation from each other gives rise to the experience of gravitating unendingly backward and forward between their polarities. What accounts for this is their very nature, which is to reflect each other dynamically. For example, one might be rapaciously speculative and morbidly fascinated about the result. But that tends to generate intolerance of the considerable demands of any of the multitude of processes that arrive there. So instead one might impatiently set up camp on some lowly ridge of spiritual experience and loudly deny the evidence of one's own eyes—not to mention everyone else's—that this is not the promised summit. The converse extreme is a nervous self-abasement that never dares lift its eyes to the horizon. It dares not allow itself to be animated by the light that irrepressibly appears through any chink in its experience. This becomes an embattled self-enclosure that only masquerades as a process. The linear progress of the wagon train across the prairie tightens into a defensive self-circling, citing some hysterical rumor of Indians. The two isolations, the cockerel on a dunghill and the mole in a hole are miserably akin.

The first Noble Truth points to life as suffering, but what many people interpret this to mean is that "life sucks." This is a serious misconception. The first Noble Truth can only be meaningful if one has looked at life from both above and below the clouds. To make sense of the Buddhist path, one needs not only to be familiar with regular unhappiness, but also to have made the most ingenious efforts to see if one can't stabilize happiness, make samsara work to one's advantage; in effect trying one's best to disprove the first Noble Truth. After engaging in strenuous efforts to manipulate reality into giving us what we want, we eventually discover that even when we get it, we don't want it for very long. Or we want it just a little bit different: more green, less red, longer, shorter, hotter, colder—whatever it is, there is always some nagging dissatisfaction. If nothing else, there's always death, which would appear to put a crimp in most people's plans.

The Buddha spoke a great deal about our dependent relationship with life, and it is a popular misunderstanding to construe this teaching as nihilism. But in authentic Tantric practice, if one knows the experience of emptiness, one can allow one's sense of identity to dissolve, to become empty. Then from emptiness one explodes into the sphere of intangible visionary appearance, instantly manifesting the form of a fully enlightened being, an envisionment. One is oneself the vision, but at the same time there is no "oneself."

A common problem of modern western society is that many people seem to be attracted to this style of practice for reasons connected with low self-esteem. There are those who thirst for emptiness as a kind of psychological suicide. They hope that in emptiness they can throw themselves away, as if it were a kind of cosmic dustbin. This interprets Buddhism as a type of mystery religion, because it can only be a great mystery how people become empowered by a process that goes by the route of disempowerment. It does not seem feasible that anyone could arise again, take rebirth as it were, as happy, healthy individuals if they had never tasted that view of themselves before. This painful and fruitless process is a sorry simulacrum of authentic Tantric practice.

Vajrayana practice is the Middle Way. It refuses both the spiritual suicide of "rational control" on one hand or "mindless surrender" on the other. The Vajrayana practitioner must stand on shifting ground—we have ceased to be the person we once were, but we have not yet become the person we aspire to be. The path is composed of authentic experiences of practice guided by the vajra master in whom we have responsibly and intelligently decided to place ultimate trust.

But this tide also has an undertow. Another common western neurosis is to idolize the lama as an infantile means of abdicating responsibility. Then the relationship becomes vulnerable to what Trungpa Rinpoche called

> ...the romantic, or bhakti, approach. You feel that you don't have it, but the others do. You admire the richness of "that": the goal, the guru, the teachings. This is a poverty approach—you feel that these other things are so beautiful because you don't have what they have. It is a materialistic approach—that of spiritual materialism—and it is based on there not being enough sanity in the first place, not enough sense of confidence and richness.[5]

I was once able to consult Her Eminence Jétsunma Kushab on this subject. Jétsun-la is the sister of His Holiness Sakya Trizin, and one of the extraordinarily scarce female lamas who are ever available to westerners. Jétsun-la told me that she had been telephoned from all over the world by practitioners who had depended on her as a source of personal advice about developing an authentic relationship with a lama. Jétsun-la echoed His Holiness Dala'i Lama's view in saying that students tended to confuse faith, or devotion, with romantic love. If one bases one's relationship with the lama on romanticism, one might follow the lama's suggestions with the expectation of yet a more intense love affair. This expectation is doomed to disappointment, which may then turn into negativity and paranoia—especially if one later comes to disparage the teacher for the advice they so kindly gave. Nowadays many lamas in the west would be inclined to voice similar caveats: do not mistake romanticism for devotion.

Taken as inspiration, stories of guru-devotion could help any practitioner to view life more positively and to develop a sense of their own self-worth and their potential within the tradition. From this perspective, what impresses us about Milarépa's story is his unending devotion and persistence. Milarépa, due to force of circumstance in his family, was encouraged to train as a black magician, and by a further chain of causes and effects went on to become a mass-murderer. He then purified his appalling karma by the dynamic means—which was his lama's compliment to Milarépa's capacity—of maintaining the pristine immaculacy of vajra relationship through extreme conditions. He felt at times both physically and psychologically tortured by his teacher, to the very brink of suicide, but he never once fell into the trap of viewing his teacher as acting demonically. The result of this practice—an accelerated path for an exceptionally rare apprentice—was realization with extraordinary speed.

But in taking Milarépa as a role model, one needs to follow a certain middle way. Spiritual practitioners almost by definition are people who long for a really difficult task, and for someone to believe that they can accomplish it. What we seek is a challenge. But to a person with low self-esteem, this story may be attractive on the basis of their desire to be punished, of feeling like a sinner expiating some great imaginary sin. Among the crowds around contemporary spiritual teachers are often students who are quietly abrogating responsibility for themselves, in an infantile dependency on someone whom they would like to view as an all-knowing, all-powerful substitute parent. This is a crude distortion of the teacher, based on the Judeo-Christian image of an omnipotent deity. In reality, the authentic omniscience of the Tantric teacher consists of total penetration and engulfment into/by the play of form and emptiness, which is the quality of every situation whatsoever. But this is a reflection of the quality of mind, not an inventory of its contents. A neurotically dependent relationship with a teacher is likely to turn into an accident looking for a place to happen.

Buddhist teachers who have personal students in their care have an opportunity to become very familiar with these problems. At the same time, every style of unenlightenment, of human neurosis, of misunderstanding the teachings, is a distorted mirror of authentic practice. From this point of view, there is nothing inauthentic about the allure of emptiness, or romantic projections, or expectations of magical cures. From the point of view of Dzogchen in particular, there is every possibility that at any moment we could allow our neuroses to relax into their own condition.

No one is necessarily excluded from Tantric practice by reason of psychological inadequacies. But the corollary to this is that the right support is needed, in terms of the Five Certainties: to be in the company of the right teacher and surrounded by the right sangha is crucial. Perhaps for every psychologically fragile person in a sangha there needs to be at least a dozen or more positively healthy individuals as role models, friends, and mentors. That might be a tall order in any spiritual community but it is not impossible. This also raises the issue of vajra relationship as a conduit of psychological health. It is certainly possible that a student who had great devotion could actually make the leap of substituting the vajra master's enlightened reality for his or her own distorted version. But unfortunately it is usually the case that the worse the neurosis the more tenaciously we grasp it. Still, in every moment there is always the possibility of letting go and opening into the vastness of the lama's space.

When Padmasambhava journeyed to Tibet at the behest of King Trisong Détsen and Khenpo Shantirakshita, one of the tasks he had to perform in this new country was to subdue numerous demonic obstacles. Ngak'chang Rinpoche commented on this in conversation, saying:

Vajrayana disciples in every place and time commit themselves to being spiritually invaded by Padmasambhava. Just as Padmasambhava traveled through Tibet and the other Himalayan kingdoms subduing demons—so too does Padmasambhava, in the guise of every vajra master, need to be invited to subdue the demons of our own psychological territory. For us as sincere practitioners what needs to be subdued are the demons of our personal agendas and the aspects of our cultural inheritance which may be antithetical to Buddhist practice. Unfortunately there now seem to be even greater demons—demons which pose as Buddhism itself. The demon who seeks to diminish the rôle of the teacher. The demon who takes refuge in the "collective wisdom of the sangha." The demon who sees fit to reconstitute dharma according to the dictates of political correctness. It is at such a time that Padmasambhava manifests as Dorje Tröllö in order to preserve the authentic Vajrayana. This approach would appear to run contrary to the mood of the times—and the well-meaning will probably attempt to promote accommodation. But the vajra master as Dorje Tröllö is not deceived by such devious appeasements. Vajrayana and its lineage holders have not arrived on these shores to make compromises with duality or to betray the non-dual heritage of dharma. If we are truly to practice, we need to abandon our need to distort Vajrayana as an exotic means of remaining entrenched in confusion.

5

THE ULTIMATE ADVENTURE

Vajrayana offers those with kindness, honesty, and courage the
chance to be real and vivid, at a time when cultural horizons are
shrinking. We cannot go forth like Lewis and Clark, in search of
the passage west—there are no such new trails to blaze on be-
half of others. The only compassionate trail left to seekers of
such high adventure is the Vajrayana.

Although there are cultural obstacles to the establishment of the
Vajrayana in the west, these are by no means insurmountable. In the
diagram of the Wheel of Life (*sridpa'i khorlo*), a Buddha is shown
teaching within each of the six realms of conditioned personality: gods,
jealous gods, humans, animals, hungry ghosts, and hell-beings. Each
Buddha is dressed and accoutred to blend in with the conditions of
each realm. They employ the style of each particular mode of suffering
to appeal to those who are trapped there, as a means of communication, to enable them to view their environment and activities in a liberated way. The vajra master has the clarity to perceive these conditions
directly, without recourse to research at the level of information.

A Vajrayana practitioner of my acquaintance once told me her
story, "The Buddha of the M&M Hell." She had been trying to lose

weight at her lama's suggestion. In fact the lama was dieting himself in order to help her, as she had reached an age when it was important for health reasons that she should trim down some 100 pounds. One day on the way to see her teacher she found herself falling into a somewhat depressed state of mind and she stopped in a store and bought a large bag of M&Ms to eat later. But when she arrived at the house where her lama was staying, she began to feel so bad about the sneaky way she'd planned to break her diet that as soon as she saw him she burst into tears. When he asked, "What's the matter?" she told him the whole story of feeling depressed, buying the chocolate, and planning to eat it in secret. He just laughed and said, "Chocolates? Well . . . you'd better bring them out then—let's eat them." And together lama and student ate the whole bag.

Buddhist teachings are always specific to the time, place, and audience. It is the people themselves, and their relative condition, who cause a buddha to manifest in their vicinity. Enlightened activity is unceasing spontaneous compassion, and compassion is intrinsically communicative. Vajra masters have always structured the path of practice in different ways according to their individual vision—and their individual vision arises in response to the specific needs of their mandala of students. This has always happened in the cultural spread of Buddhism, as it passed from country to country in earlier times, so we can have confidence in this precedent. Some western lamas and Tibetan lamas teaching in the west have made certain changes to adapt to the cultural milieu in which they find themselves.[1] For example, many lamas have relaxed the formality inherited from the more hierarchical Tibetan culture. Some lamas prefer their disciples only to make prostrations to them on ceremonial occasions such as empowerments, practice, and teachings, rather than whenever they meet, which might be in the local library or supermarket.

Ngak'chang Rinpoche and Khandro Déchen are definite about limiting prostrations to occasions when they give ritual empowerments. As lamas within a *yeshé cholwa* (*ye shes 'chol ba*; crazy wisdom) lineage, their approach to teaching has been highly individual. They present their disciples with what they describe as "eccentricity rather than crazy wisdom"—and this wisdom-eccentricity always appears to remain deliberately within the bounds of what is considered ethical by mainstream society. They hold themselves accountable to their students according to the Five Precepts, and to the injunctions of the Khandro Pawo Nyi-da Mélong Gyüd (*mKha' 'gro dPa bo nyi zLa me long rGyud*), while also making it clear that their students must never judge any other lama according to such criteria. Ngak'chang Rinpoche and Khandro Déchen wrote:

> The function of yeshé cholwa or "crazy wisdom" is so important to our lineage, and to so many other lineages of the Nyingma tradition, that we can neither manifest it nor fail to manifest it. We cannot manifest it because we lack the realization required. We cannot fail to manifest it because to do so would be to deny the inspiration of Khyungchen Aro Lingma. We are therefore merely eccentrics rather than true examples of yeshé cholwa, and in that capacity we can only attempt not to bring discredit on our lineage through manifesting behaviours which would give rise to doubt as to our motivation. That we live in this way and according to these criteria is due to our insignificance rather than to any "ethical" virtue we may possess. Mahasiddhas such as Trungpa Rinpoche, Dungsé Thrinlé Norbu Rinpoche, and Kyabjé Künzang Dorje Rinpoche are not bound by the small fishbowl of our vision, and therefore have no need to restrict their enlightened effectiveness.[2]

If realization consists of delicate insight into the nature of every situation, and the ability to behave with consummate appropriateness, then the vajra master could decide to work within the limits of any chosen conditions whatsoever. In the west, the lama could display a willingness to integrate the teachings with society, by overtly abiding by the laws and moral code of this time and place; or, equally, not. Padmasambhava himself is said to have stated: "My mind is as vast as the sky, but my activity is as refined (discriminating) as grains of flour." He was describing the wisdom and compassion aspects of realization.

If Vajrayana is ever to become functional in the west, we need to adapt ourselves to it rather than attempting to change it to accommodate our prejudices and neuroses. Our culturally based conviction of the ultimate value of individual freedom (by which is meant the "freedom" to follow one's samsaric rationale) is one thing we need to examine. We have been indulging this supposed freedom all our lives: has it brought us any closer to liberation? Do we have any reason to believe it ever will?

Another consideration is the style and content of western psychological dysfunction. Many—perhaps even most of us—reach adulthood with unresolved issues left over from early childhood. These are then projected onto the vajra master in the form of rebelliousness, dependency, fantasy romance, or any number of other unhealthy modes of relating. For many westerners, a good foundation (*ngöndro*) for a life of Buddhist practice could be a few years of psychotherapy—as long as it was a form of therapy that did not engender "therapy addiction" or encourage indulgence in the sovereign importance of "me."

Here in the west, even Sutric Buddhism seems to require a prior foundation. Therapy would be a practice that could be suggested to those people who are currently looking to Buddhism to solve a variety of psychological problems. Buddhist teachers may be happy to offer refuge to all kinds of people, depending on how the idea of refuge is viewed in their individual traditions.[3] But at the same time it seems more and more that teachers have to be prepared to recommend that a proportion of those who come to them take a look into the broad spectrum of available psychotherapies. It is important, however, that one does not take refuge in therapy as being a level of truth by which dharma can be judged. Therapy should be viewed instead as a method for removing some of the obstacles and hindrances to Buddhist practice.

It is also important that therapy does not create or reinforce a sense of narcissistic self-obsession. There seem to be two different general results from long-term therapy. The form of therapy that is counter-productive, from a Buddhist viewpoint, is whatever converts people into "ancient mariners", doomed forever to buttonhole strangers, grabbing them by the lapels to lay their story on them, like pouring emotional vomit into somebody's coat pocket. In the nature of vomit, the perceptible solids always seem to have a hideously familiar and repetitive nature. I am referring to the way that "therapy" of this type leaves clients convinced that it really is their parents, siblings, teachers, employers, friends, partners, and children who are responsible for their unhappiness and unpleasant behavior. This myth of self-justification bears out the withering wit of the Viennese critic Karl Kraus, who observed that psychoanalysis is itself the disease it purports to cure.[4] A good result of therapy would be if people concluded it prepared to take responsibility for their own lives. The karma of seeing oneself as a victim should have been substantially eroded.

There could be some practical guidelines for therapy that would be a genuine foundation for Sutric Buddhist practice. Applying the same principles as for the Tantric ngöndro practice, it would have to resemble the path of Sutra itself and incorporate real Sutric practice. In the same way, training for any activity resembles the activity itself and to some extent is the thing itself. Thus it would theoretically be possible to obtain the results of the whole path from the foundation exercises alone.

The nature of Sutric practice is renunciation, letting go of the objects to which one's problematic emotions attach. In Sutra, the teacher is supposed to be of the same gender as the student. This is meant to prevent any frisson that might arise from gender difference. So the Sutric therapist (for a heterosexual client) would also be of the same gender. The therapy would have a number of aspects through which the client would cycle. One would be talking, in a rational manner, about life problems—no visualizations, no role playing, just analysis and reconstruction, using one's day-to-day mind. Another aspect would consist of formal silent contemplation of the results: meditation with form. The third part would be manual labor, which could also be performed as a single-sex group activity. This last would have several valuable functions: as a preparation for living in a closed community (monasticism being the ideal framework for renunciate practice); to cultivate the sense of self-reliance and self-sufficiency which goes with that; and as a prelude to meditation—because strong physical exertion, as everyone knows from mundane experience, produces a non-conceptual state of mind in which it is quite difficult to do much thinking even if one should wish to.

The preparation for vajra commitment would have a great deal to do with gaining an understanding of its principle and function, and taking responsibility for oneself as a person who is able to make promises and keep them. One needs to have exhausted the desire to see oneself as a victim, and have enough resilience to be able to tolerate challenges to one's personal version of reality. It is useful in this context to have a path of graduated levels of commitment to a lama and a lineage, with each new level being explicitly acknowledged by both student and teacher.

In this context, I ought to describe the model called apprenticeship, which has evolved in the Confederate Sanghas of Aro since 1979, through the intense care of the lineage-holders, Ngak'chang Rinpoche and Khandro Déchen.[5] It is a four-level system of involvement in the lineage. At the first level, of uncommitted exploration or window shopping, there are open teaching events: evenings, whole days, and weekend seminars or retreats, which anyone may attend. This enables people to receive teachings directly from the lamas, and on residential weekends there is the opportunity for private interviews with them as well. Issues arising from life crises can then be introduced as a major practice, equal with meditation itself.

In time, some students may come to identify with the lineage as their primary spiritual home, the Buddhist tradition with which they feel most in harmony. They may then apply to be accepted as personal apprentices of a particular lama. This is a state of spiritual friendship, and, to whatever extent is needed, it can also be somewhat of a therapy. To apply for apprenticeship requires studying and discussing with one's prospective lama a lengthy informational document (currently running at several thousand words) about the lineage, and its definition of the freedoms and responsibilities that can make spiritual friendship really work. This is followed by a probing questionnaire and application form.

Apprenticeship is the first stage at which taking refuge as a Buddhist is said to be essential. In this lineage, refuge is never given as a blessing without commitment. It has an element of challenge; it is a door to the future, and is viewed as lifelong. It closes off doors to the past; it calls into question every kind of non-Buddhist refuge and serves to sever one's commitment to other conceptual allegiances, whether religious, philosophical, psychological, or political. This issue is not always well understood by prospective apprentices, and indeed some long-term Buddhists seem confused by it as well. The point is that, in taking refuge, we are saying that from now on this will be our context, this will be the overarching paradigm, the pattern that contains all other patterns.

We are committing ourselves to the path of dharma (as it is) because we have come to believe that it is a method for coming to experience undistorted reality. After this we can no longer judge dharma by the standards of any other belief, philosophy, or identity. We are Buddhists, practitioners of dharma. We are not American Buddhists, German Buddhists, western buddhists, women Buddhists, working-class Buddhists, or gay Buddhists. We are Buddhists who happen to be American, German, western, female, working-class, or gay. It is vital to understand this distinction.

After a minimum of five to seven years, an apprentice may seek to take ordination in the lineage. This is a life-long commitment to represent the lineage and wear the robes of the respective style of ordination.[6] It has a second stage, when, after further years, ordained disciples may be deemed to have enough knowledge and experience to teach. They are still only known as lamas-in-training, and they may not necessarily aspire to have personal students or to be teachers of the public in the conventional sense. The full title of lama depends on accumulating the traditional three-year retreat. This means solitary retreat, as contrasted with the collegiate style developed by Jamgön Kongtrül in the last century, but not necessarily accumulated in a single block of time. This reflects the Dzogchen style of following the appropriate practice, rather than the Tantric style of practicing according to a set formula. Both ordination and teaching depend on examination, as well as retreat, the results of practice, the endorsement of one's personal tutor, and more unusual foundation requirements such as pilgrimage.

The sangha is quite small by design, in order that the lamas can have a close relationship with each student, and somewhat specialized; it is a purely yogic lineage that comes directly from the Tantric Buddha Yeshe Tsogyel. Over the last five hundred years, this style of practice has become uncommon even in Tibet. Perhaps because of this we have been at pains to develop a structure that has a chance of surviving for generations. Taking the "paradox highway," we have prioritized the medium in which we swim above our own place in it. We preserve the white skirt and uncut hair (*gö-kar chang-lo*; *gos dKar lCang lo*) of the yogic community or White Sangha tradition, the outward signs of difference from the monastic (red) sangha. These symbols have fallen victim to persecution at various times in Tibetan history, and have become somewhat exotic by their rarity, especially in the west. But the west is already the home of Christian, Jewish, and Muslim non-celibate clerics, so there may be a fertile field for Buddhist equivalents—if that is what Buddhists desire.

There will soon be a greater choice of lamas living and teaching in the west, including younger Tibetan lamas with multi-cultural experience. There is also much interest in seeing greater numbers of female lamas. Westerners who have received the appropriate training and are recognized as having the necessary qualifications and potential could be further encouraged and trained specifically to teach. Teaching could begin in circumscribed areas of knowledge or experience, and grow in a modular fashion. It could start within the sangha, the lineage, or the school, and later expand to the general public. Some Vajrayana lineages in the west are already training teachers in just this way; it would seem to be a matter of common sense.

The lamas of the future could be traveling less, and spending more time with the groups and individuals who host them. It would be possible for their students to get to know them better, and vice versa. That could be the ground for a meaningful, responsible decision about whether this could be an appropriate personal teacher—for the time being, for a lifetime, or beyond. And, conversely, teachers could more openly encourage their potential students to take responsibility for their choices, in the way that all the classic teachings insist. Communities of Tantric practitioners such as these could become centers of overt psychological health, which would be a powerful living endorsement of the Tantric path.

For more than a decade now, an informal discussion has been alive inside many sanghas concerning the teacher-student relationship in general and how best to preserve its particulars. Every practitioner needs to come to an individual understanding of his or her own experience and how it fits into the wider context of Vajrayana in general. The issue of how to preserve the authentic Vajrayana in its transition to the west is a matter on which we as tantrikas have an obligation to develop personal views, and, if not conclusions, then a piercing experiential awareness of our shortage of conclusions. In the ringing words that Kyabjé Chhi-'mèd Rig'dzin Rinpoche once said to me: "You are a Tantric man. You must Know." Those who understand the real meaning of Vajrayana are obliged to defend the role of the vajra master, in whatever way presents itself.

We must always keep it in mind that the conditions of vajra rela-

tionship are set by those who confer it, not by those who request it—
and those who confer it, confer it as it was conferred to them.
Ngak'chang Rinpoche states:

> As Lamas, Khandro Déchen and I are servants of the Nyingma
> tradition. Our concern is for the living embodiments of the Ti-
> betan Buddhist lineages. Those who consider themselves Tibetan
> Buddhists need to think carefully about their attempts to seduce
> lamas with their "integrity". . . . In the 19th century and even the
> earlier half of the 20th century, there used to be a social function,
> designated "breach of promise," whereby a young lady could sue
> for damages if trifled with by a man who made promises he did
> not keep. We will not pursue this analogy with regard to the
> Lama, apart from pointing out that breach of promise is now a
> joke—people can say whatever they wish and not be held ac-
> countable to anyone. We find this depressing. We do not feel that
> this is the way to build a better world. If we cannot keep promises,
> we should attempt not to make them. But, of course, if we do not
> make promises . . . Vajrayana becomes inaccessible. Vajrayana is
> only accessible through promise. Vajrayana is not just another
> process. The Lama, the vajra master, is central to Vajrayana—
> and without the vajra master to abuse our fixation with duality we
> are merely the slaves of dualistic rationale.[7]

We are all prisoners of our time and place to the extent that we
mistake the prejudices and assumptions of our own culture for reality.
Sincere practitioners need to ensure that this cultural prejudice is
acknowledged and destroyed in the only effective way it can be:
through practice that is informed by the view of Vajrayana and not by
other agendas. Those western buddhist teachers who have suggested
reducing the role of the teacher in order to make Vajrayana more
democratic perniciously misunderstand this crucial point.

At this juncture, it may be useful to conclude with some selected statements from Ngak'chang Rinpoche and Khandro Déchen's introduction to this book:

> Vajrayana has no political bias—its frames of reference lie completely beyond the dictates which govern the ordinary ordering of society. Vajrayana does not deny the validity of democracy or egalitarianism within secular society. Vajrayana simply speaks of the natural right to be free—even to the extent of being free of the myth of freedom. Vajrayana presents vajra relationship as the final portal of freedom. Through this portal we enter a dimension in which we are able to question the otherwise unquestionable—our narcissistic determination to maintain the illusion of duality.

Vajrayana holds that everyone is equal in terms of their intrinsic vajra nature—their beginningless enlightenment. Vajrayana holds that all beings are equally worthy of compassion. However, Vajrayana does not hold that beings should be limited in their capacity according to the lowest common denominator allowed by those who wish to restrict human freedom. To restrict the freedom of beings in order to enforce an artificial equality is to shrink the quality of life—to homogenize the enormous range of sentient potential to fall within legislated parameters. This is a particular brand of democracy which lends itself to the insidious evolution of despotism.

> If one cannot be free to give up the sovereignty of one's narcissistic rationale, Vajrayana becomes meaningless. If we fail to recognise the compassionate nature of vajra relationship as the heart of Vajrayana, then we are left merely with a prosaic esoteric pastime.

With the advent of Vajrayana as a functional spiritual development in the west, we have a rare opportunity to accept the challenge of maturity rather than regress toward infancy through the agencies of emotional incontinence. Vajrayana offers those with kindness, honesty, and courage the chance to be real and vivid, at a time when cultural horizons are shrinking. We cannot go forth like Lewis and Clark, in search of the passage west—there are no such new trails to blaze on behalf of others. The only compassionate trail left to seekers of such high adventure is the Vajrayana. We should think carefully about the risks of adventure, and about those who took such risks in the past. Nothing is gained if nothing is ventured—and if nothing is risked, nothing is won. We cannot create a safe adventure of a safe Vajrayana.

The spiritual stories we love to hear are all about the wild yogis and yoginis, the mahasiddhas, the crazy wisdom masters—not the safe and predictable saints, even acknowledging their sainthood. This book is for those who love these stories. It is meant as encouragement to leave the comfort of dubious safety and blandness and enter the heart of the adventure that is Vajrayana. It is only through contact with the tiger-like aspect of the vajra master that we can come to discover our own tiger nature, and to manifest that for the benefit of others.

6

COMMON QUESTIONS
ABOUT VAJRAYANA

This chapter consists of an interview that concerns a wide variety of issues that have become topical among people who attend teachings and retreats offered by the various Vajrayana traditions. Nga-la Rig'dzin Dorje candidly discusses some key points with Ngakma Shardröl Wangmo, who poses questions from her own experience of teaching, and from observing the situations in which many newcomers to Vajrayana find themselves.

NGAKMA SHARDRÖL WANGMO: On the issue of finding a teacher in the first place: people seem to have some understanding of checking out the potential vajra master before entering vajra commitment, and also of listening to different teachers. But many seem to find the process increasingly fraught. As a result of articles in Buddhist magazines and an atmosphere among some Buddhists in the west, there seems to be a sense of anxiety and paranoia around the role of the teacher.

NGA-LA RIG'DZIN DORJE: That's a shame. Unfortunately nothing can happen unless one is able to relax, so a paranoid mind-set is not the place to start. Perhaps people need to take a long-term view. If something, anything, is going to be a spiritual resource, it should have the potential to be life-long. One could be reborn into it in this life . . .

NSW: That could have a very particular meaning for Christians.

NRD: I'm not shy of using the phrase in a Buddhist context. We too are born again; so that we may eventually die within the stream of that rebirth. One of the blessings of a spiritual path is to be able to die in the atmosphere of a particular knowledge of birth and death—in the way they are expressed according to the tradition. For a Vajrayana practitioner, this stretches into contemplating the possibility of being reborn with a connection to the same tradition in some future life. So if one is thinking that far ahead, one needs to take one's time. One needs to undertake one's research with openness and intelligence.

NSW: Doesn't that lack a sense of urgency, though? What about keeping awareness of death in mind as something near us all the time, as something that could happen at any moment?

NRD: Also true—paradox lies at the heart of Vajrayana. It is implicit in the *Heart Sutra*. There is no Tantric topic that one can pick up without being obliged to contemplate opposites simultaneously. That's a challenge, in a world in which fundamentalism is a great temptation—even Buddhists may find themselves vulnerable to it. Openness and intelligence might be the emptiness qualities of one's pursuit. But their method reflex would be finality. Unless one is capable of making a final decision in life, an ultimate choice; one is running the risk of dying "on the hop" between traditions. That being the case, what is going to be one's refuge in the bardo between lives? Who ya gonna call? Ghostbusters! But that is actually why taking one's time would be highly pragmatic. *Festina lente*, hasten slowly; in order that one does not overlook, or waste, or mutilate what might turn out to be one's long-term refuge. Instant gratification is endemic in our society: to take one's time could feel like a kind of death in itself. One could realize in that time-taking that one was on the brink of dying to all other spiritual alternatives. The Buddhist view—pluralistic non-dualism, resulting in atheism—is unique among the world's traditions. There is a Tantra of Dzogchen *sem-de* in which it is said that the Dzogchen teachings exist in thirteen different solar systems, but from what I've seen they are an extreme rarity even here.[1] So, dying to the alternatives is a rite of passage that is really quite necessary if one is to experience one's commitment to Buddhist refuge as being meaningful. Taking time to look properly allows our consumer instincts to wither: the dance of death to the muzak of time, under the toxic fluorescence of the spiritual supermarket. We would be making an agreement with ourselves simply to be there, relaxing in that situation. It's a delightful paradox of form and emptiness. The more we can embrace the form of a tradition, the more we can relax about having made our decision. And in relaxing, we become open to perceiving its spacious universality. That's a powerful catalyst of change—it's one reason why people often have quite significant experiences in meditation at the very beginning of their involvement with practice. When you don't know what to expect, you're very open-minded, ready for anything, but doing nothing in particular. That's an amazing achievement in itself.

Being a new parent, I think of the process as similar to finding a suitable school for your child. When you take your child along to check out some establishment, you may have different agendas operating at the same time. As a parent you may have issues about academic standards and examination results, options, extras, costs, policies, discipline, and so on. At the same time you're eyeing your child to see how he or she is reacting subjectively to this environment—and you also have your own subjectivity. You're observing decor, atmosphere, the behavior and appearance of the other children, even the smell of the cooking and the toilets, and the echoes of shouting in the corridors. So there is urgency. There is urgency because you know that you are committed to a decision-making process. Lack of urgency would be allowing yourself to float in a daze, just going along for the ride. There's a difference between taking your time when that time is being gainfully employed to make a meaningful decision, and taking your time because there's no sense of importance.

Relying too much on one tool to the exclusion of all others—the intellect—is quite a common mistake. Now, Buddhism is the only religion I know that teaches that it is useful to be intelligent; that formulates teachings in terms of how they might be cognized by people of differing capacities. But what is valuable for a student of Vajrayana is the enjoyment of one's intelligence; bringing concept-consciousness within our sensorium.

NSW: That sounds like a phenomenally difficult practice.

NRD: You're right, in that it could be understood in terms of an important result, right there. Initially however, I'm suggesting something quite concrete. It means, for example, meeting with the propositions and arguments of the teachings in the same way that one would register the sights, sounds, smells, and savors of, say, a Buddhist temple.

NSW: But isn't that exactly what a "dharma tourist" does, stepping off a bus somewhere in Asia?

NRD: I don't mean stepping off the bus just long enough to take a photo before hitting the next historic beauty-spot. The attitude behind that is, "I'll appreciate it later, when I get the prints back from the lab and I can match them up with the blurb in the guidebook. I don't have time to get involved right now, I'm on a tight schedule."

NSW: So, what would getting involved really require?

NRD: Enjoying the play of paradox, the movement of logical steps, the spaciousness of a comprehensive set of terms, the strength of unbreakable conclusions, the depth of an individual's insight. All in all, the richness and fertility of language. I have a particular appreciation of my root teacher, Ngak'chang Rinpoche's, prolifically fecund use of English. To use the power of language so as to communicate something so effectively to individuals, that is compassionate activity in itself; it is that which is liberated by unbreakable insight. One could read a book as a tourist of philosophy; or as a guide to one's hometown. It needs to be emphasized here that, typical of Vajrayana, there is tremendous sensual richness and potency involved with this research, and Tantra is based on transmuting sensuality. That's both its power and its danger.

NSW: If it's transmutation, how could that be dangerous?

NRD: You could make a mistake. You might be merely kidding yourself that transmutation is occurring. Self-indulgence is also possible. At the atomic level of perception we experience the senses in the moment, instant by instant. The senses are doorways—the doors have a more transitive function than that of windows. You can move into the experience of nonduality through your own senses. This is what makes Vajrayana, to my mind, the most optimistic expression of spirituality that has ever manifested in human culture.

NSW: Frankly, that could sound just a little too good to be true.

NRD: But it's not easy—and, to begin with, not necessarily pleasant. First, you have to come to an agreement with yourself that you really will experience your experiences. It's necessary to learn the taste of not accepting, not rejecting, not manipulating. Without this, you can scarcely begin authentic Vajrayana practice. And please note: this is a point of departure that is beyond the outcome of psychotherapy. You can't transform what you're not experiencing. Returning to the child-at-school experiment, and broadening out what I was saying before about concept: when looking for a spiritual path, you have to start by enjoying such things as the sound of the language, the cut and color of the robes, the style of the decor, the æsthetic of the thangkas and statues, the movement of the letters on the printed page, the fragrance of the incense, the taste of the ritual food offerings, the sound of the instruments and voices, the mood of the characteristic sentiments, the aptness of the philosophy. That sense of psycho-physical enjoyment has to be there, because that in itself is an empty form.

NSW: Can you say more about how this works in practice?

NRD: That really *is* the practice—right there. Anything else is going to sound even less concrete, more abstruse, and further from what is practicable.

NSW: It might be helpful to hear how it sounds anyway.

NRD: Well, whatever your realized space might be—any clearing that you've succeeded in transforming out of the sensory jungle—

that is the space where you can meet the with the Mind of the lama. That would be the all-important experience called transmission. Space is always the same space: the same for all phenomena, the same for all beings. Buddhism is pluralistic, not monist. It's pluralistic because phenomena are infinitely variegated. Phenomena proliferate and change without limit. Phenomena are only "one" in emptiness. Monism denies the evidence of the senses, and suppresses that which makes Vajrayana so vividly functional. The empty aspect of the Mind of the lama is nondual with form—in other words, it is the state of realization. Entering the empty state in the mandala of the lama—

NSW: Could you explain the idea of mandala in this context?

NRD: It's like saying: in the presence of, or in the company of, the lama; to whatever extent, in time and distance, you may feel that presence radiating. If you can enter the empty state of the lama within the mandala you have a chance to experience the enlightened state of the lama yourself. This holds true whether we're talking about a formal occasion, typically a Tantric empowerment, or the completely informal personality display of the Dzogchen master, without any outer signs or symbols.

NSW: Could you say a bit more about this experience of transmission?

NRD: Transmission is the state of total openness in which we allow the lama to function as the enlightened being he or she actually is. You see, usually our pattern is either to attempt to deify the lama or to attempt to convert the lama into an ordinary person. Both of these strategies are born from our self-protection; protection from the necessity of change. Deifying the lama means refusing any kind of abrasion. It is to put him or her on such a high throne, at such an exaggeratedly respectful distance, that there is no danger at all that the lama might, terrifyingly, stick his or her head into the cesspit of your existence and say, in kindly puzzlement, "Ahem, excuse me, but how exactly would you relate this ongoing disaster to your everyday practice?" So that's a way of closing down, or burying your head in the sand. Maybe some future gTértön will have visions of a body of practice protected by the terrifyingly wrathful ostrich-headed dakini; but, to date, I've not heard of ostrich behavior as such being a spiritual practice. This could also be called blissing out. It might look like devotion, but actually it's just another way of hiding from the lama. I should say at this point, that when I speak of deifying the lama as being a problem, I am not falling in with the crass criticism of devotion described with the linguistically bizarre phrase, "over-idealization of the teacher." I simply mean that the vajra master is a buddha—not God Almighty creator of the universe with the capacity to change all your distressing circumstances and cure your dog of halitosis.

NSW: And if you attempt to convert the lama into an ordinary person?

NRD: Then you can only receive what you could receive from an ordinary person. There is a saying that runs: "If you see your lama as a buddha, you obtain the blessing of a buddha. If you see your lama as a bodhisattva, you obtain the blessing of a bodhisattva. If you see your lama as an ordinary person, you obtain the blessing of an ordinary person." But in the example we were just discussing, you might run the risk of seeing the lama as a demon. You might even find it highly convenient to assert that publicly. You might cite it as the grounds for breaking all manner of vows that you held with the lama. But for transmission to occur, you have to be able to experience your lama as a buddha. And, actually, that ability in itself is none other than transmission. For the disciple who experiences his or her lamas as buddhas, every moment in their presence—or out of it—is transmission.

NSW: Could you explain the difference between this and "blissing out"?

NRD: Well, first, experiencing one's lama as a buddha is based on practice, not fantasy.

NSW: So how can you tell which is which?

NRD: It's true, there is also the potential of making a mistake, a downfall, which would be the corollary of what we've been describing. That would be that you fail to move into the essential knowledge of nonduality, but instead into the isolated idiosyncratic experience of psychosis. For a long time, your view of yourself is likely to flip back and forth between the two. And that's only reasonable. Because, if you never failed to adapt to that knowledge, you would be the holder of the result already. Where do you go for confirmation? Your only possible recourse is to the lama. What prevents that from being circular? Only the realization—the insight, kindness, and clarity—of the lama. If there is realization or not—only time and practice will tell. That's why taking time to experiment is necessary; but with the urgency in the moment that we talked about at the beginning. Meanwhile—study and practice go hand in hand. See what genuine Buddhist books have to say about how the path develops: by contrast, be informed about what cult activity looks like. Be discriminating. Challenge the fundamentalist dumbing-down of spirituality. Second, transmission is not necessarily euphoric. It may be electric, but not euphoric in the sense of becoming somewhat brain-dead. In the blissed-out state one has retracted the intellect. In genuine devotion the intellect still functions but is open to being overridden at any moment. There's a big difference. In Vajrayana, faith needs to be unified with intelligence. Faith without an awake, inquisitive, alert, lively sense of basic intelligence can be somewhat useless.

NSW: Can you say a little more about the word *faith*? It seems to be quite problematic for some people.

NRD: Yes, but I think that I can do no better than to quote Khenpo Sonam Tobgyal Rinpoche, one of the lamas at Pema 'ö-Sel Ling, the retreat land of Lama Tharchin Rinpoche, near Santa Cruz, California. I'd just like to read you something from the text of an interview conducted with Khenpo Sonam Rinpoche in the fall of 1999:

> I very much liked what Ngak'chang Rinpoche was saying: You cannot just take any one thing from Buddhism into your life; you have to take the whole thing . . . Vajrayana practice depends

86

so much on [the] guru and student relationship. It is the faith and devotion to the guru that is what ultimately transforms us. That faith and devotion turns into wisdom, which is an unbroken realization of the wisdom of awarenes—rigpa, which is the inseparable quality of Samantabhadra and your teacher. So you have to have that faith and devotion to your teacher. Ngak'chang Rinpoche points out that there are certainly cultural forms of Buddhist practice—cultural differences—but that the principle and function of Buddhism must be clearly understood. The vajra master is part of the principle and function of Vajrayana; they don't exist separately. When you are practicing, there is vajra pride in your practice, a pride in your practice which you do not understand. This pride itself, if you interpret it, is actually some kind of discriminating wisdom. Then you understand; and with it you know how to analyze, how to investigate your teacher. That pride itself becomes a wisdom—this faith and the devotion itself becomes the wisdom. Some people believe that it is some kind of blind faith. I know that some people have this blind faith, but it is not that.

I really feel that faith and devotion are the main practice of Vajrayana. If you lack that, then there is no fruit in your practice. Without a teacher, you cannot attain enlightenment. You have to depend on a teacher. Depending on a teacher means that you have to have this faith—and that this faith itself is the wisdom. It is said in the Sutras: "Do not rely on the teacher, but on the words of the teacher." But you have to rely on the teacher when you are in Tantric practice. Then it is said that it is not only on the projected meaning of the word, but on the hidden meaning of the word—and also not on the conceptual consciousness but on the wisdom reflection of your mind—you should rely on that. That itself means guru; that itself is the guru.

Faith and devotion are one kind of antidote which purifies or eradicates all of the emotions. If you do not have a teacher, you can become very prideful and arrogant. When you have pure faith and devotion, it means that you have pure awareness or pure recognition. It is called pure perception. If you have pure perception, you could express it as dharmakaya. You could also express it as sambhogakaya or nirmanakaya. We are talking about guru—you have a guru who is a nirmanakaya of the Buddha. Talking on the nirmanakaya level, that is the practice of Tantra. To experience that which you experience through pure perception is enlightenment, and the pure perception practice is gained through faith and devotion . . .[2]

NSW: One question I hear from a number of people I meet is this: "What happens if you make a really serious commitment to a lama, and then you break it? For whatever reason, maybe you think you've made a mistake, or you can't handle that particular style after all, or you go off the rails and do something you think is so terrible you can't live with yourself or the lama anymore.

NRD: Well . . . that would actually be based on a lack of honesty, which would have been there from the start. If you make a serious commitment and then you think you've made a mistake, then there's a question you could put to yourself about that—though not many people do, it seems. The question is: "How could you consider this new idea, that you've made a mistake, to be any more serious or valuable than your initial idea, the commitment you made, which you thought at the time was to be final and binding? If you have come to doubt that previous moment, how can you not also doubt the present moment?"

NSW: That sounds blindingly reasonable; but by the same token, it could be viewed as being possibly a little . . . frigid?

NRD: You could say it's too cold. You could equally well say too hot; or even—by virtue of indicating the Middle Way— too tepid. Because those aesthetics only reflect whether we respond to emptiness with aversion, attraction, or indifference. We are certainly liable to .

respond in one of those ways because this is a direct challenge to the pretended primal priority of our precious personal process.

I would say that the doubt, or the idea of having made a mistake, should be considered as one of the bogus get-out clauses common to our culture. We are taught that our momentary feelings should be pre-eminent, and that we must follow them. Some people claim that what they are doing is loyal to the necessity of their personal process; but this appears to mean investing in its unendingness. The only personal process in Buddhism is towards the person becoming empty of fixed identity; not towards synthesizing interminable new personae, even spiritual personæ. That's the great danger of misunderstanding the Sutric path, right there: artificial Buddhist personality. I have known two people in particular who have claimed to be men of honor on the basis of following their feelings at the expense of their vows. It was interesting that in both cases "honor" had very little to do with their behavior. It would seem that claiming to be a man of honor is a popular stance for those afflicted with narcissistic personality disorders. What was the other question?

NSW: Going off the rails . . .

NRD: Ah yes, doing something you think is so terrible that you can't live with yourself or the lama anymore . . . Well I have never encountered that, actually. Usually such people justify themselves right down the line and blame the lama for everything. Some of them even go on to write books about it and hit the lecture circuit with all manner of unlikely stories that are later proven to be fallacious. It's tragic that people are able to make a name for themselves on the basis of sensationalizing their dysfunctional personalities. It strikes me as distinctly worrying that there is such a cult of the vow-breaker nowadays. How can one possibly use having once been a monk or nun as a credential? But several western authors have endorsed themselves in this way. If we are so ready to welcome "the one who got away" as an authentic "one of us"—what does this say about our own relationship with commitment, honor, morality? How demonic a consumer culture is this, in which we look for the get-out clause before even reading the rest of the contract? In other walks of life this kind of unprincipled opting-out would not be tolerated. People can actually be subject to litigation. But the teachers such people malign have no interest in defending themselves. Dharma needs no defense. Anyone who was actually sorry for breaking their vows would be given considerable help by their former lama. The lama is always deeply concerned with helping people to keep their vows. It is said that vows can be repaired even up to three years after breaking them. Kyabjé Künzang Dorje Rinpoche has even said that within Vajrayana there is no limit to the time in which one can repair one's vows. But as time goes on it becomes increasingly difficult. One can judge, up to a point, from the way that it becomes more difficult in ordinary human experience; if someone has betrayed an intimate relationship, withdrawn from a business partnership, or defaulted on a financial commitment, for example. But nothing is impossible. It's all in the mind of the disciple. All one has to do is recognize one's slipperiness, and express the wish to overcome it. If one has a desire to seek spiritual health, then opportunities usually present themselves. The glory of Vajrayana is that everything can be transformed.

NSW: What would you say about the traditional description of the consequences of breaking vows, like the hell realms?

NRD: The outer explanation can sometimes take a form that could be perceived as esoterically lurid. Because we are in the west we tend to be obsessed with the nihilistic view that nothing outside our experience has validity, such concepts appear to call for either unreasoning faith or a deliberately acculturated credulity—so there would seem to be no purpose in pursuing this theme here. The inner explanation, however, can be more mundane. That's a typical paradox of Tantra; because what that means is that it calls for a more refined perception, one capable of finding the extraordinary in the very appearance of the ordinary. In this case, the outer explanation might have something to do with the most vividly dire penalties for broken vows—repercussions from transcendental beings like protectors. But an aspect of the inner explanation would be how you feel in yourself, how you deal with the fact that you now cannot fully trust yourself—ever again. If you can give up something that once held such immense meaning, how can you ever trust yourself again? This is the hell of never again being able to find spiritual value, or the hell of taking refuge in your own neuroses—because everything else is the object of paranoia.

NSW: It sounds bad either way. What about vajra hell?

NRD: Ngak'chang Rinpoche mainly explains that in terms of a psychological state. He has often said that vajra hell is the hell of "taking refuge in terminal dualism." It's a paranoid state in which there is absolutely nothing to trust but the convolutions of one's own perceptual anguish.

NSW: So what would be the difference between vajra hell and regular hell?

NRD: Well you see, people in ordinary hellish states are quite desperate to get out of those hells—it's just that the methods they use are counterproductive. Because it's actually the desperation itself that is keeping them in hellish frames of mind. But vajra hell is hell with a horrible twist. What's so appalling about vajra hell is that one tries to remain in it, in order to escape from the lama and from the possibility of enlightenment.

NSW: What would make that seem like any kind of desirable way to live?

NRD: Let's imagine a person who had previously taken refuge as a Buddhist. Refuge means expressing confidence in being able to dissolve one's dualistic fixation. Then this man (let's use the example of a male rebirth) met a certain lama. Over a period of years, he had a very good experience with this lama. This experience appeared to be enough to give him the sense, from his own reflected experience, that this lama had unmistakable realization. This led him to the conviction that with the guidance of this lama, his own realization would be possible. This experience, shedding all ideas about the limitations of what might be possible for a human being, was powerful. So, in the traditional way, he made a binding commitment to remain with this lama until becoming completely enlightened and he gave the lama the great Tantric mandate: "Please be as you actually are." That is to say, "Please accept me as a vajra student." Now, can you imagine the mind of this man after defaulting on such a commitment? He would be living in hell—even if his situation actually seemed comfortable in the mundane sense.

NSW: But if his experience was so strong, so convincing, what would make him change his mind?

NRD: He took himself seriously. He took his sense of progress seriously. You see, the terms of vajra commitment make it clear that things can only go wrong in the perception of the disciple. (I use the term *disciple* here to emphasize the profundity of the difference in status that vajra relationship represents.) If the disciple withdraws from viewing the vajra master with pure vision, and enters into denial of the experience of transmission, what is left for him as a refuge? All he can do now is invest in continuously justifying himself: anything to avoid looking into the face of his own evasiveness, the source of his self-torment.

But, and here's the catch, this doesn't mean he can go back to square one; the point before he ever embarked on the path. When he was at square one he was at least attempting to lead a decent sort of life. Even if his experience was not always happy or successful, he had the idea that his chosen path ought to lead in that general direction. This has all changed, and in a terrible way. Now, bizarrely, he's obliged to invest in being isolated in his misery. He has to do this in order to justify blaming the lama for ruining his life. If he ever stopped his self-torture long enough to start taking responsibility for his life again, he'd be unable to avoid remembering that this is where he came in before, and remembering where that once had led. Being his own spiritual guide hadn't worked before: that was why he empowered the lama to be the vajra master in the first place. But now he cannot permit himself, even for a moment, to consider the fact that the lama might have been even just a little bit right. That would be too painful to bear: it would, in fact, be hell. So the way out of vajra hell looks, from the vajra-hell perspective, as intolerable as hell—regular hell, that is. There's a certain realism in that all right. But what cannot be glimpsed from vajra hell is the fact that, back in regular hell, at least the thought of happiness could arise once more. With enormous help from the vajra master, that struggling aspiration would have the chance to be translated back into a path of practice. Liberation could again be possible. That's therefore another way of describing the awfulness of vajra hell: from that viewpoint, re-connecting with authentic practice again would look appalling—it would look like hell.

In vajra hell there are two choices—it's either hell or it's hell, and the lesser hell is always seen as the greater hell. The lesser hell of accepting that one invested in one's narcissistic self is seen as more painful than the vajra hell of taking refuge in one's own terminally dualistic rationale. The lesser hell can be alleviated, but it would mean swallowing the claws of the toad.

NSW: Is that a Tibetan saying?

NRD: Er . . . no, Sicilian actually. It means being prepared to absorb the very nastiest part of the most horribly unattractive situation. Here, it corresponds with the Tantric idea of ripping out the heart of self-justification. It gives the same sense of the physical unpleasantness of the operation. Regular hell could change. Reconciliation and purification might even be possible. But in vajra hell, to prove that he was right, that student has to keep the lama permanently in the wrong. This means that in order to be happy he has to remain tortured, a vilely inverted kind of Tantric paradox: hence vajra hell. So vajra hell is a state in which you actually dedicate yourself to remaining in hell.

NSW: Forever? Could that really last the rest of your life?

NRD: At least. The problem with vajra hell is that it is the most massive of all reference points. Vajra hell is different from the six realms of karmic vision in that it is somewhat less impermanent. It cannot change without some massive and prolonged shock. You don't want it to change, so naturally this makes it less likely to change. If you were to sustain that for long enough in your life, it would lead to problems of a different order, complications within complications. For this unfortunate man, the more his life circumstances changed, the less relevant this gnawing conflict would be in terms of the life he was trying to live. The emotional center of his life, this buried guilt and anguish, would have to be deeply repressed. So he would become slightly strange. We're talking about more than just having a chip on his shoulder: we're talking about paranoia, compulsive self-justification, narcissism, and sociopathy. His need to justify himself would cause him to deform his life experience to accommodate his preferred image of himself and this would corrupt all his personal relationships. It would be like an inverted reflection of the god realm.

NSW: Isn't the regular hell realm an inverted reflection of the god realm?

NRD: Not in the sense I mean. You see, all the six realms exist in the same continuum of ordinary neurosis. They are characterized by the different speeds and intensities with which people manage their unenlightenment. They are the bizarre lifestyles whereby people try to make unenlightenment workable, more comfortable. In the god realm, one expects to be comfortable forever, immune from any kind of comeback, always on the receiving end of an unaccountable free lunch, untraceable in the computers of the cosmic IRS. Vajra hell is an inverted reflection of this in the sense that in vajra hell one nurtures one's grudges forever, one never ceases to feel victimized for having had to pay such a high price for one's deviancy, one feels the IRS has always had one's number from the very beginning . . . So it's a comparable eternalist fantasy. Such a person would also wish to pull others into his pit, but if he succeeded he would get no joy from his success. That's why it is usually considered best to avoid vow breakers—unless one's practice is sufficiently advanced.

NSW: A lot of people ask about this, so I was wondering if you could explain what the difference is between the practice of taking our life circumstances as the teaching of the lama, and some kind of psychotic state. I mean, when people have psychotic delusions they sometimes read messages and significance into everything, don't they? So what would be the difference?

NRD: The practice of taking one's life circumstances as the teaching of the lama is not meant in the sense that everything that happens has an explicit meaning. Say a construction worker drops an egg sandwich on you from a great height, and this awakens you to the realization that the lama is suggesting you become a vegan. Or does it mean he thinks you should eat so many eggs that you become constipated? What's wrong with this approach is that it's a backward step into a pre-Buddhist refuge, a refuge in your own solipsistic rationale, interpreting the world according to your comfort zone. That approach is actually one of monist superstition, a borderline psychological coping strategy. It's true, that joke of some ancient philosopher: "superstition brings bad luck"; or you could say "bad judgment."

NSW: Borderline?

NRD: In the sense that it could be nudging at the envelope of sanity, in just the way you suggested. Life circumstances are not teachings in the sense of conceptual messages. But they could be ultimate teachings, in the sense of transmission, introductions to a different world of perception, every moment potentially replete with inspiration: moments of positive inspiration, but also moments of negative inspiration—obviously a rather harder practice. This is the meaning of the outer Tantric refuge in daka/dakini. When these moments of inspiration blow you away there is no you. When there is no superstition of separate identity anymore, in that moment there is nothing to prevent union with the phenomenal world. The senses and the sense field are found to be in ecstatic embrace. Experience itself becomes the sexual consort: daka for the female practitioner and dakini for the male.

NSW: What do you do when students come to you, and they have serious psychological problems?

NRD: I have to express my appreciation for what Baker Roshi said in reply to this question, according to an interview I read. His answer was, "I send them to the psychotherapist." The difference is that I cannot imagine myself having the authority to "send" anyone anywhere. But with my own students, I am often able to make suggestions: sometimes strong suggestions. In the case of someone urgently requiring not just a psychotherapist but maybe a medical psychiatrist, obviously the suggestion would need to be quite emphatically strong. That would accord with the Tantric vow of never failing to act in an emergency. That vow would have to override any more laissez-faire working methods one might normally express through mere suggestions. The purpose of apprenticeship, according to our system, is to test out the effectiveness of the lama's suggestions. I have found myself recommending therapy from time to time. If I were continuously living close to those students, so that I could see them every week, perhaps I could figure in the role of therapist myself. There is no particular problem in having this as part of one's range of activities as a lama.

NSW: But doesn't Buddhist practice itself have the capacity to take people beyond their psychological problems?

NRD: Oh yes, indeed: especially inner Tantra. Dzogchen in particular integrates everything with awareness, through a practice called *trek gcod* (*khregs gCod*). Trek gcod means "cutting through;" in quite an explosive sense. This cutting-through is not just a dainty snip of the tape, like the queen opening a museum. It's as if one's consciousness (the skandhas, if you prefer to use the language of Sutra) were a viciously constricted, densely compacted bundle; like a bundle of dirty laundry, maybe. How the cord came to be around the bundle is not described, only the method of its liberation. Actually, nobody tied the cord around the bundle: keeping oneself bundled-up is our self-constriction. If one finds one's experience to be bundled up, then there is a remedy. If one's experience is relaxed, in the moment, then no remedy is necessary. If one severs the cord around it, the bundle doesn't just flop apart: it springs out wildly in all directions, and the constituent items collapse in their own space. Then one finds something truly remarkable. Nothing has been lost or wasted. All the things one possessed in the bundle have been retained; but there is no need to bundle them together any more in order to prove their existence. So, of their own nature, they are liberated. Before, there was no experience of space in the bundle, just the tightness of the constricting band. Now, there is no band, the bundle is spacious, and everything exists in a relaxed state. One finds that nobody has severed anything: one has simply allowed self-severance to occur. There is nothing to enclose, nothing to exclude, nothing to sever, no tool with which to cut. When spaciousness is the ground, there is nowhere to fall and nowhere from which to fall. When spaciousness is the method, there is no path to follow. When spaciousness is the result, there is nowhere to aspire. There is nowhere to go and no "one" who is going.

There is nothing in ordinary mind that cannot be liberated through these methods. Concepts are allowed to self-liberate without intervention. But this is where one has to look again at an important principle: half is the practice, half is the person who practices.

NSW: Where does that idea come from? Is that Tibetan?

NRD: Actually no, it's from Ngak'chang Rinpoche and Khandro Déchen. It's also a matter of my own observation, both of myself and others. I have been deeply impressed—actually inspired—by the ability of particular students to blast through quite severe psychological handicaps (verging on a need for psychiatry) through dedicated persistence in these practices. They were able to keep up their practice because of their certain knowledge that, however difficult it might sometimes be—and it is often described as the hardest possible thing—the alternative of remaining as they were was far, far worse. And quite possibly these were students who felt a karmic connection with these teachings, such that it seemed to them to be absolutely the right way to approach their difficulties. The results have time and again confirmed to me how stunningly appropriate it can be to introduce these teachings publicly nowadays. On the other hand, we have all known people with the most banal but lingering attitude problems, who have been incapable for decades of settling into any one stream of spiritual practice of any description, or who are uninterested in any such thing, or who become evasive at the point where the authentic practice begins to bite. This is often the point at which students decide that they are teachers themselves and have no further need of a lama. I have seen this happen. In the case of one man, he simply backed off from all real involvement with his teacher and set himself up as a guru in his own right. He became so inflated with his own sense of importance that he was unwilling to acknowledge aspects of his behavior which were so decidedly antisocial as to have suggested the appointment of a psychiatric social worker. The more his lama tried to help him through his difficulties, the more antagonistic he became.

NSW: I have been informed in quite a determined manner that the guru is something alien to true Buddhism, and that the Buddha never taught that one should put oneself in the power of another, that one should always check the reality of the dharma for oneself. I think the person to whom you refer has made such statements.

NRD: Yes, I believe you're right. He's one of a number of advocates of the "inner guru." It is certainly true that in the Sutras, Shakyamuni Buddha taught that one should always check the reality of Dharma for oneself. There can be no argument with that. However, Shakyamuni Buddha also gave teachings regarding the prime importance of the lama. This idea about the guru being alien to true Buddhism is merely a piece of propaganda based on ignorance of both the Sutras and Tantras. The very notion of "true Buddhism" is a concept invented in the west anyway. In the early part of the twentieth century a group of English armchair intellectuals decided that they wanted a religion that "made sense." They settled on Buddhism—or rather, I should say on certain aspects of Buddhism. Their preference was for a hybrid of Theravada and Zen, in which they could throw out whatever there was of each that did not appeal to "the rational mind." It's interesting that the western buddhist teachers who are currently involved in this anti-guru campaign are little different in their approach and orientation, apart from that fact that they have added a pulp-fiction version of Dzogchen to the Theravada-Zen mix.

The main problem with this is that these anti-guru agitators are often respected by people with little or no knowledge of the actual teachings of Buddhism. It's for these people that I am mainly concerned—for those who are so new to Buddhism that they can be taken in by smooth speeches catering to western cultural prejudices. The guru or vajra master is the very foundation of Tantra. The idea is that one has benefited in practice from relating to the lama as a spiritual friend. The benefit takes the form of the power of transmission. So one is not being disempowered by the lama, one is not helpless at the hands of another. Quite the contrary: it is from this source that one's own ability emanates, according to one's capacity and that of the lama. There is nothing alien to Buddhism about that—nothing alien to Vajrayana Buddhism, at any rate. It is the lifeblood of the tradition.

These teachings and practices would not be available to us today if they had not been passed down through successions of relationships of just this type. When you are in vajra relationship, you have a job, a mission, actually. It is your training for the real job, which begins when complete enlightenment is reached. At that point one is supposed to become supremely useful in the world. In a similar way, you can be supremely useful in vajra relationship too, in enacting the vision of the lama rather than following the dictates of your own rationale. You are actually assuming greater responsibility, not shirking it or lapsing into some zombie trance. It is only possible to fulfil a role like that if you are a mentally healthy, mature, balanced, experienced, responsible person, able to take care of your own life in such a way as to make it a vehicle for working on behalf of others. Then, relationship with the lama reveals itself to be the highest samaya vow. It makes redundant any daydreams of praise or anxiety about blame for your activities, any lingering hope of success or nagging fear of failure. To keep that one samaya is profoundly liberating in itself.

NSW: It seems these days that many people at the forefront of "western buddhism" seem to be suggesting that the spiritual friend is a more "appropriate" model for the west.

NRD: There have always been people seeking to undermine the extremely individual relationship between vajra master and disciple. It is predictable that such people would like to replace that relationship with a far-reaching institution instead, subject to their own authority. In relating to the vajra master you only have to experience the qualities of a single person: the teachings are presented through emptiness. In spiritual friendship, you are required to be comfortable with hierarchies and committees and written regulations: the teachings are presented through form.

NSW: I have heard some western buddhist teachers state that there has been an over-emphasis of the vajra master. Or actually "over-idealization" was the term they use—you referred to it earlier. They are saying that a vajra master must always be judged according to how he maintains the precepts. They say that gurus such as Tilopa and Marpa do not exist today, and so to teach in the way they did is no longer possible. What do you make of that, in view of what you've been saying?

NRD: To take your latter point first: I would be inclined to inquire how they would know whether lamas like Marpa and Tilopa existed today or not. How do they arrive at such a preposterous declaration? Was His Holiness Düd'jom Rinpoche not the equal of Tilopa or Naropa? Was His Holiness Dilgo Khyentsé Rinpoche not the equal of Tilopa or Naropa? And what about the sixteenth Karmapa? There have been so many mahasiddhas . . . And today we have Kyabjé Künzang Dorje Rinpoche and Kyabjé Dodrüpchen Rinpoche . . . There are so many wonderful lamas such as Dungsé Thrin-lé Norbu Rinpoche and others who are less known.

Ngak'chang Rinpoche commented on this once and, if I can paraphrase, he said that this idea of gurus such as Tilopa and Marpa not existing today is a highly devious proposition. It allows the traditional vajra master role to exist, but only in the past. It's devious because, of course one has to allow that role to exist: to deny it would be to contradict the essential nature of the Vajrayana. Yet the argument disallows the vajra master role for all practical purposes by saying that no one alive today has the realization to actually live that role. In that case, R.I.P. Vajrayana. Ngak'chang Rinpoche pointed out that this kind of argument is pietistically divisive. He said to me:

> If Vajrayana can lead to liberation in one lifetime then the Lamas who lead us toward that goal must have realisation. If the Lamas who lead us to the goal of realisation in one lifetime do not have realisation then they cannot lead us. If the Lamas have realisation but are not the equal of Tilopa and Naropa, then how is realisation within one lifetime possible? If realisation within one lifetime is not possible then Vajrayana is not Vajrayana.

Ngak'chang Rinpoche commented that in terms of this analysis we can either take Vajrayana seriously or not. If we take Vajrayana seriously then we have to be able to work within its parameters. If we say that its parameters are unworkable, then we cannot pretend that we're practicing Vajrayana. Therefore there can be no such thing as egalitarian Tantra or democratic Dzogchen. Unless one sees one's lama as the equal of Tilopa or Naropa, liberation within one life makes no sense at all. This is fundamental. For a practitioner of Vajrayana, there can be no argument with this.

Vajrayana is not for everybody. Those who do not feel themselves to be adequate to the challenge would do well to consider the adage, "If you can't stand the heat, get out of the kitchen." For people who talk about over-idealization of the vajra master no vajra master could ever manifest as the focus of practice. The would-be student's incomprehension would be a karmic obstacle between themselves and the tradition. That is why some lamas of the wisdom-eccentric style would sometimes actually drive away students before they even had the chance to make a connection—for their own good. Even to hear about the existence of such lamas could be disturbing and even angering to some people. As I said, I read the magazines. The disturbance, anger, and self-serving opinions of those who feel antagonized by the mere existence of Tantric teachers is alarming to read. So is the implied complicity of the editors who print such material without comment. Such teachers only manifest in the life-streams of those who have the karmic development to make use of them. But in the final analysis, in vajra relationship there is no higher authority than the vajra master anyway, so it doesn't matter what people say about it: the vajra master is the heart of the Vajrayana.

In the Nyingma School, every practitioner views his or her own lama as Padmasambhava or Yeshé Tsogyel in person, and it's completely normal to hear Tibetans refer to their lamas that way: for instance, Lama Tharchin Rinpoche speaks often about Dungsé Thrin-lé Norbu Rinpoche as being Padmasambhava in person. Ngak'chang Rinpoche often refers to Kyabjé Künzang Dorje Rinpoche and Jomo Sam'phel as being Padmasambhava and Yeshé Tsogyel in person. It's only uncommon in the west, I think, because although we are used to hearing teachings on guru yoga and devotion, it is not always understood as being absolutely central to the path of Vajrayana. Some teachers are maybe somewhat reluctant to spell this out, except in terms of describing their experience of their own teachers—and so students don't always get the point.

Lamas assume whatever personality is compassionately effective for their particular students. This might or might not manifest as the wisdom-eccentric behavior of the great stories of the past. A lama might even appear strikingly different to different people, and this is also traditional. One Nyingma lama, who is known for his extraordinary behavior, gives empowerments that make my hair stand on end;

but an unfortunate man who attended one of these same empowerments described it as being similar to listening to someone reading from the newspaper. There was evidently no auspicious connection there.

Tantric lamas might appear to be decidedly peaceable citizens, without for a moment compromising their power of transmission. Ngak'chang Rinpoche can sip his customary morning decuple espresso while gazing wordlessly into space—and for me, radiate transfixing crazy wisdom. Khandro Déchen can sit silently on a sofa and the whole room seems to emanate from her as if she had just manifested it. They are gentle people who place great emphasis on courtesy and kindness yet they are not predictable or "safe" as far as my own delusions are concerned. That can be an empirical experience. In their presence, the substance of the ordinary phenomenal universe appears to have been replaced with some quality that is not anything in particular but seems to be responsible for everything. I would say that experience and view my lamas as being Vajrayana in person.

Then again, an alternative style might be to exhibit wrathful or unconventional energy in the ancient manner. But this would also be compassionate because it would demonstrate the unbroken power of the lineage as a living inspiration for those who can work with it. As to keeping the precepts, how can anyone tell who is doing what? Naropa found his lama, Tilopa, throwing live fish into a frying pan. By clicking his fingers, he was sending them to a better rebirth. Who knew? Padmasambhava himself committed a murder when he was still a boy Prince Siddhartha abandoned his wife and child. For some people, it would be dangerous even to hear about such things. A Tantric or Dzogchen master might be keeping the precepts according to their essential meaning, rather than their usual outer meaning. The mother and child whom Siddhartha abandoned, and the mother and the child whom Guru Rinpoche murdered, these represent cause and effect: in a word, karma. The Buddhas embark on the path of practice beyond karma, which is one of the descriptions of Dzogchen. Who could perceive that? Who except someone with equal realization? It's a field of enormously vivid and vital contradictions. Dagmèdma, Marpa's wife, might have come across as a pious Tibetan housewife, yet there are traditions in which she is recognized as a Dzogchen master, and that she was responsible for furthering the Dzogchen aspect of Milarépa's training. Did any of Marpa's other disciples even notice her? What do you think? The bottom line is that people who have dogmatic attitudes about the vajra master do not have much hope of recognizing vajra masters even if their paths were to cross. So to that extent they will always be safe. Or they will always be impoverished—whichever way you prefer to look at it. But even when they merely hear rumors, it seems to upset them. That was how it came about that some *yidag* (hungry ghost, or intellectual) professorial type attempted to murder Milarépa.[3] And that kind of thing was going on right up until this century.

NSW: This is an unpleasant question, but it's something that some people do wonder about: at the end of the day, how can we be sure that the vajra master isn't a cult leader?

NRD: It might be more useful to ask, "At the end of the day, how can I be sure that I am not a cult follower?" Ironically, with the question of cults, the student is the only person who can allow or frustrate the possibility of a cult coming into existence. It depends entirely on the way the student relates. If the student is in a weak, dependent, fantasy state, superstitiously projecting power onto the lama and relating to the lama as a substitute parent, then that student is a member of a cult, no matter how impeccably the tradition defines itself, or how formally it describes the relationship between lama and student, or even how the lama actually behaves. It is said that one cannot be a Buddhist teacher unless there are students who grant one the scope to manifest in that way. Likewise, one cannot be a cult leader unless one is confirmed by cult devotees. Hitler's single talent in life was the ability to express passionately the worst of what was already in peoples' minds.

NSW: So the next line of the argument asks: what about the idea that introducing students to the role of the vajra master is letting children play with fire or electricity, because they have no concept of the danger they're in?

NRD: The vajra master is not looking for children. The vajra master is not even looking for adolescents. The vajra master is looking for mature adults—people who have at least reached the age of consent. Isn't that an interesting expression, "the age of consent?" It means becoming mature enough to know when we can give ourselves away. Whereas it's adolescence that can be supremely selfish. The lama cannot make use of callow dependents in carrying out the activities of the lineage. The vajra master needs active, energetic, creative, socially functional adults. A parent takes care to keep a child away from the most obvious threats, and the lama does not expose the student to vajra relationship without all manner of checks and balances beforehand. But even so, there's no ultimate guarantee. The vajra disciple could be a psychopath—cultivating distorted proclivities in secret. One could not blame the lama in such a circumstance—because even Shakyamuni Buddha had Devadata.

NSW: Devadata?

NRD: Devadata was the Buddha's own cousin, but he was the student who tried to kill the Buddha and set himself up as a teacher. Ngak'chang Rinpoche once commented that it was the great compassion of Shakyamuni Buddha that gave the example of Devadata to all future teachers. One could not expect to be free of a human blight that even Shakyamuni Buddha encountered. Interestingly enough, Devadata also presented himself as a man of honor ...

The compassion of the lama resides in taking people at their word. That word is called *damtsig*, or samaya, the sacred oath. Vajrayana makes that sacred oath possible for people, and the vajra master cannot protect himself or herself against those who are not enlightened and therefore still susceptible to narcissistic delusion.

NSW: There are people who are asking how to distinguish between a teacher who is abusive and who possibly has little realization and a teacher whose acts are beyond judgment. They worry that the very act of making such a distinction would seem to break samaya. They describe it as some kind of double bind—we have to be able to make a distinction, and yet we can only judge an enlightened being if we ourselves are enlightened. Can you comment on this?

NRD: This question doesn't really make much sense from a practical perspective, and I think it's another example of a synthetic, deliberately divisive hypothesis to sabotage the role of the vajra master. The time for making distinctions comes before one makes vajra commitment. During that period there can be no breakage of samaya because the samaya doesn't yet exist. There would only be a double bind if one entered vajra commitment as soon as one met a lama—and that never happens. No lama ever forces a student into vajra commitment. But it is amazing how some students will insist on taking vajra relationship as the model from the very beginning, even when the lama emphatically rejects that. These are the students who, at the same time as insisting on the impeccability of their devotion, will vociferously resent all the lama's suggestions as an abuse of their tender fledgling sensibilities. That's attempting to put the lama in a double bind. It's the student's abuse of the teacher: a topic insufficiently discussed, I would say.

NSW: I've heard that some western buddhist teachers want to establish a system of validation for who is an authentic teacher and who is not. What would you say about that?

NRD: If you experience transmission, it makes no difference at all what anyone may say to the contrary. Vajra relationship means finding oneself outside such considerations. Transmission is a mature experience; and to take a lama who may not be especially valued elsewhere, or who may be virtually unheard of—takes considerable maturity.

NSW: Can you define the "new age", and why we need to make an effort to separate Buddhism from it?

NRD: The "new age". . . Beyond saying that it's "feel-good spirituality" it's not easy to define. There's no straightforward definition because the "new age" is based on the most non-rigorous synthesis of anything and everything. Loosely speaking, the "new age" is an out-growth of the pop-culture comprehension of Hinduism that informed Theosophy. Actually, one could say that it's a watered-down version of Theosophy with degraded inheritances from Jung melded in for good measure. From a Buddhist point of view, "new age" is an amal-gam of monist eternalism and dualist eternalism. It's a form of eter-nalism that opts for monism or dualism according to whichever seems most comfortable. And whenever one of them proves momentarily uncomfortable—which eventually it always will, in falling short of describing our essential nature—then, presto, one can always shift one's ground and take refuge in the other. So the "emptiness aspect" of the "new age" is intellectual dishonesty. Its "method aspect" is an indi-vidualistic approach in which the ethics of personal responsibility that accompany true individualism have been abnegated. To put it bluntly, the "new age" encourages people to design their own "spiritual path" from whatever religious elements seem most agreeable and flattering to their egos. One would therefore have to say that the form aspect of the "new age" is ethical dishonesty and moral cowardice.

NSW: So, from a Buddhist point of view, the danger of a "new age" adaptation of Buddhism is that monism, dualism, nihilism, and eternalism—the four philosophical extremes—corrupt the very fabric of the teachings.

NRD: Exactly; although the "new age" runs a little short on nihilism—unless it's the nihilism of "nothing having meaning for me unless I agree with it." One certainly finds that in the expressed hos-tility to Vajrayana that I mentioned I've noticed.

NSW: You seem to use the expressions "Tantric lama" and "root lama" almost interchangeably. Are they the same thing?

NRD: Yes and no. The Tantric lama or vajra master, is the oper-ative mode within the Vajrayana: that is to say, Tantra and Dzogchen. One could more properly say "the Vajrayana lama." The "root lama" is the Vajrayana lama whom one chooses—and by whom one is cho-sen—to function in the role of vajra master. One usually has only one root lama. The root lama is one's personal lama. One may have many lamas in terms of masters from whom one has received teachings and transmissions, but the root lama is the one who choreographs one's personal practice. Lineage holders such as Ngak'chang Rinpoche may speak of having had a number of root teachers—in his case, five—but refer to one of them as the "heart master."

NSW: In the west we seem to place a great value on personal independence. What would you say to people who believe that vajra commitment is an abdication of responsibility for making one's own life decisions?

NRD: I had a favorite uncle who used to say: "If you can't make decisions in life you're not even a mensch." I suppose you could characterize this condition of being unable to make decisions as a steady state of adolescence. In other words, we assume that life will go on forever and that there will be endless time to change, endless possibilities, and eventually we will select the right one. Society seems content to see people remain in this state for as long as possible, because then they continue to be optimistic consumers. This is a notable feature of the Kali Yuga, according to traditional teachings: life-span gets shorter, in the sense that psychological development becomes truncated. Someone who has not yet become a mensch, a decisive person, has not reached "Buddhism square one." Square one would be an acknowledgment of the first Noble Truth, that one cannot find perfect security in life; meaning, in dependency on life .

These are lessons learned in pain and they are necessary lessons. If we're trying to relate to the vajra master as the "good mother/father/friend/lover" we never had, this will not work. The vajra master eventually dismantles all projections, so it becomes impossible to hide from responsibility. If disciples try to avoid taking responsibility, the vajra master might refuse to give them any advice at all. The lama might even ask them for advice—and follow it. The vajra master role is utterly superb in terms of harpooning, lampooning, and lambasting duality and all dualistic contrivances, as long as the disciple has devotion. The idea is that, in becoming a disciple, we are prepared to participate in bringing to life the lama's vision of useful activity. So, we are open to advice and direction—and changes of direction—and are constantly prepared to lend our resources to that. This is not dependency: it's possibly more like joining an elite military corps; becoming "an officer and a gentleman." Trungpa Rinpoche, as far as I can interpret his writings from outside his lineage, appears to have held the line as an actual serving officer, under orders, in the vajra guard of the Rigden King of Shambhala. We may have to be extremely self-reliant and mature to take on projects that might be outside our experience or outside our limited view of our own capabilities. But because of our commitment, failure is unacceptable; or at least failures that are the result of not applying ourselves sincerely. Success means that we transcend the idea of our own limitations. This, of course, is the essence of Tantric practice—dissolving our experience of ourselves into emptiness, and then erupting into a new dimension of existence. This is worlds apart from any state of psychological inadequacy.

NSW: When you say that the vajra master dismantles all projections, do you mean that he or she will eventually contradict them, be different from what we're expecting?

NRD: Yes, absolutely, because the vajra master is going to destroy our neurosis by any means possible. The vajra master is the living presence of realization, which is beyond dualistic personality. Therefore any projection we have *has* to be wrong. By definition it would be a reflection of our own needs, inadequacies, comfort-zone, and so on. It is the vajra master's compassion to take us beyond neurosis, and we give the vajra master carte blanche to use whatever method is going to achieve that result. This will be different for different students. Some people can transcend themselves on a mere suggestion. Some have to go through horribly painful and repeated experiences of the failure of their rationale. Some don't need anything from the vajra master at all: their state of constant openness and readiness is effective in itself. This brings us to the subject of devotion: that is the essence. I was interested to read an interview with Khenpo Sonam Tobgyal Rinpoche in which he quoted Shakyamuni Buddha as saying: "The end of the path is reached solely through devotion."[3] In these terms, vajra relationship is the fast track. That's why it can be dangerous. It's dangerous if one is not completely mature and genuine. If one's involvement is merely a collection of neurotic fantasy, it will fall apart at some point and fly back in one's face.

NSW: Since you said that any projection onto the vajra master is going to be wrong, could it ever be possible to see the vajra master without projection?

NRD: I would say that would be a quality of the experience of transmission: without projection, without concept, without definition—simply a fierce frisson; the real meaning of bliss and emptiness.

NSW: Going back to what you said about psychotherapy as the foundation practice for Sutra, do you think that Buddhist practice can be helpful in dealing with mental illness, or would it just be confusing for people who haven't yet formed what Freud called a healthy ego?

NRD: I've had some experience with this but not enough to be able to say anything scientifically respectable. But I would say that for people who are emotionally fragile, the most important part of the triple refuge is the way in which the lama manifests through the sangha. That means they should be surrounded by a group of happy, mentally healthy, kind, friendly, normal people who are actually practicing, and who have real devotion toward the vajra master. Then there would be less of a tendency for these people to see themselves as "great yogis or yoginis" and get lost in fantasy. Within a gray area of dysfunctionality, somewhat depending on the group average, they would be still accepted as part of the sangha. Ngak'chang Rinpoche and Khandro Déchen's vision of apprenticeship is important in this respect. If the lama says this person is a Vajrayana apprentice (*gé'trug–dge 'phrug*), then everyone treats the person as a gé'trug. This is pure vision in action. It's a self-fulfilling prophecy, and can actually be effective in helping the person to feel better and become more stable.

NSW: I wanted to ask you about the way you expressed the first Noble Truth: that one cannot find perfect security in life. Would you say that the experience of suffering comes from taking the experience of samsara as reality?

NRD: I think that the idea is to get beyond experiencing lack of security as something devastating. That's the great advantage of the human realm, the mixture of pain and pleasure. Pleasure, in that we can have a sense of humor about it, we could even laugh at our own misfortunes. That's the humor of the human realm. Lack of security can have an undertone of pleasurable frisson: teetering on the ledge between self-preservation instinct and death wish. Imagine your life's work being destroyed in a house fire. Remember what it was like when you realized the big relationship was over; or if you maybe lost the best job you ever had. You might oscillate between depression, devastation, and moments of rising, giggling exhilaration, because this disaster also spells freedom. We die in the end, you know… And life is riddled with valuable opportunities that can facilitate the integrated emergence of that knowledge. It is knowledge of which we are deprived by "conventional wisdom." If we spend our entire lives skipping from one crumbling rationale to the next, when and how do we accumulate the experience of allowing everything to fall apart? Because that is what we have to be able to do in the face of death. To be able to stare into the face of the total loss of everything with which we identify only serves to make us stronger. That is a typical paradox of form and emptiness. It could be a terrifying experience of emptiness, or a serene experience of emptiness, or even a realization, a non-dual experience of emptiness and form. Being blasted apart by insecurity can leave one utterly open. In this state of openness, the entire unbounded universe floods in. Having nothing one has everything. Having no "thing" as a reference point, one actually owns everything. Being nothing, one is everything. Being no "thing" as a focus of self-reference, one actually is whatever one perceives. Being nobody, going nowhere, one is inseparable from everybody everywhere.

NSW: Vajrayana seems to be so much less known than does Sutrayana. People seem confused by the idea of ordained Buddhists who drink alcohol and eat meat, not to mention subjects such as vajra relationship. In the past, and for some teachers in the present, Tantric vows and practices were kept secret. Do you think this is useful?

NRD: My feelings and thoughts about this have changed over time, so it's probably only appropriate to offer a snapshot of them in the present, which may also change. I feel that I have certain responsibilities, and I'm happy to take my bearings from them: responsibilities to my lamas, to my apprentices, and in general to the Aro gTér lineage. We are incredibly fortunate to be in receipt of these extremely concise teachings, which are a complete path in themselves. My idea is that people should always be devoted to their own tradition, and respectful of everyone else's. We should see all other spiritual practitioners as reflections of ourselves. If that's not possible, what on earth is the point of dedicating one's practice to all sentient beings? Oh, you mean all sentient beings except for . . . ? My experience has been that when people take an interest in our particular Vajrayana tradition, it's never because we are able to justify ourselves intellectually. It's because we are—on a good day, with a following wind—ecstatically happy just to be doing what we're doing. As for secrecy, I don't make the rules on that: I teach what I have been permitted to teach, and within that I use my best judgement to introduce people to what will support their practice and not be an obstacle. Then I take a look at any Buddhists who turn up in courses and try to get an impression of how the tradition has helped them, or if it has been put across in any way that has been counter productive. I can definitely learn from that myself, as a lama. But I can't legislate for trans–Himalayan Buddhism in general. I know that His Holiness Dala'i Lama has said that many secret things need to be made public nowadays just so that they can be kept alive.

He has also said that it is good to speak about Vajrayana now in order to dispel the many misconceptions that have arisen due to flagrant popularization of Tantra in the west. He said that the time for secrecy is over, because it is better that people learn the truth. This doesn't mean revealing secret methods such as *togal*, the rainbow body practice, but speaking about the information that has already appeared. The Tantric vows themselves have been published; and one could see that as a valuable initiative, inasmuch as it adds solid fuel to the hot air of discussion. Ngak'chang Rinpoche and Khandro Déchen have always been very careful not to reveal anything publicly that is not already available. They have always made a point of helping people to understand the teachings of Vajrayana in terms of elucidating upon what has been published. Teaching beyond this has always been reserved for their own students and those who have taken vajra commitment. In the west, lamas have a responsibility to make it clear to their students what they are actually capable of practicing, and what needs to be kept in the drawer until they appropriately mature. But this implies a closeness in relationship between teachers and students that is often not the case. Without the possibility of conscious vajra relationship as a path, I don't see how Tantra can survive as a method of realization. Without the relationship with the vajra master, Vajrayana would dwindle into just a colorful philosophy or a spiritualized branch of psychotherapy that makes use of spurious "archetypes."

NSW: I've noticed that some people who are interested in Tibetan Buddhism seem to find the ceremonial aspect—robes, prostrations, all the ritual that surrounds a Tantric empowerment—to be problematic, or at least hard to relate to. Do you have any advice for people who are perhaps attracted to a lama and the teachings but who find the ritual aspect to be an obstacle?

NRD: If someone is interested in a lama, that should mean being interested in what the lama does. This might mean letting go for a while of one's colossally inflated sense of the importance of one's rationale, or aesthetic. That means agreeing temporarily that one might not be the best possible judge of the right components for one's spiritual path. It could be remotely possible that one did not know everything.

I would say that Tantra is culturally alien to people in some respects but maybe not in as many respects as they might at first imagine. Remember, at one time it was culturally alien for the Tibetans as well. But the student does have to find some workable point of contact with the teachings. Then, if there's enough space for the lama to work, the more problematic areas can wait until later. At the least, I think the lama can ask the student not to indulge in too much judgment. In Vajrayana there is a concept of the student needing to have certain qualifications too, not only the lama. If there's a real relationship between them, then the student ought to be able to find enough inspiration to accept some process that the lama feels to be valuable, at least provisionally. So I would return once again to the idea of transcending one's limitations.

NSW: Because you teach a lot in Europe, most of your students are not native English speakers. How has this influenced the way you present the teachings?

NRD: It casts me in the role of the alien, which is sometimes helpful. Let us experience the awkwardness of communication as a sign of the fragility of cultural structures. Let us celebrate our common sentience and more, beyond the possibility of interpretation or misinterpretation. On the other hand, I am limited to students who speak enough English to be able to express their emotions. That is crucial, or else they become terribly frustrated. So my apprentices tend to be well-educated people. That means they may have benefited in their lives and careers from having a good intellect; but conversely, they may also quite possibly have experienced the torments of intellectualizing about their emotions. But that becomes an eminently workable nexus of forces, through the symbolism of the five elements. The five elements are a vast topic, but one which can be a simple medium of communication. This is probably why the five elements have become quite central in what I do. It's a teaching in which people of any nationality can recognize themselves, with delight and with exquisite pain. That definitely facilitates a bond of some kind. Likewise, Dzogchen sem-dé contains many explanations of form and emptiness that present opportunities to say the same thing in many different ways, so there too is a culture of communication. The teachings of Dzogchen are often called essential; but like those compressed Japanese paper flowers, you can drop them into the water of any country, and they will expand in exactly the same way.

NSW: It seems that in the west we simultaneously have an over-valuation of rationality at the same time as a kind of naïve desire for magic and mysticism. In terms of Buddhism, some people have problems with the concept of tulkus and reincarnation, but others just swallow it all in a kind of haze of fuzzy romanticism. I was wondering how you deal with these things as a lama.

NRD: Well, there's nothing like a healthy quota of confusion and mixed motivation. In the role of lama, I wouldn't attempt to deal with these issues head on. Why spoil such a lovely atmosphere of fascination, uncertainty, contradiction, and irritation? In Vajrayana people have to experience things for themselves. For each individual practitioner, things are simply as real as they are real. If one has had no experience yet, then the experiment simply continues. One starting point is as good as another.

NOTES

Introduction: Buddhist Traditions and Vehicles

1. In the lineages that emanate from Yeshé Tsogyel, she is spoken of in the same terms as the Vajra Guru Padmasambhava himself, and they are regarded as having performed their teaching activities jointly.
2. "Entering the stream" refers to a stage in the path, according to the Sutra tradition.
3. Tib. *zhi, lam, dré-bu* (*gzhi, lam, 'bras bu*).
4. The four schools of Tibetan Buddhism are Nyingma, Kagyüd, Sakya, and Gélug. The Nyingma is the oldest of these.
5. It is called "display" because the personality is empty. This concept of "empty personality" is almost unknown in western psychology except as a pathology. It is interesting to consider how this might have been different had Carl Jung lived long enough to have heard teachings on Vajrayana direct from authentic sources. He might have undermined his own ideas of a perfectable self, which is one of the poisonous roots of the "new age" with its cruelly naïve optimism and fascistic spiritual materialism.
6. Dzogchen is divided into three series: sem-dé (sems sde), the series of the nature of Mind; long-dé (klong sde), the series of space; and me-ngag-dé (men ngag sde), the series of implicit instruction.

Chapter One: Opening

1. Ngakpa Chögyam, *Wearing the Body of Visions* (Ramsey, NJ: Aro Books, 1995), p. 144.
2. Ibid., p. 178.
3. Tibetan meat-filled dumplings, either fried or steamed.
4. A fond personal memory from the late A'pho Rinpoche's *gompa* (retreat center) in Manali.
5. People have often been tempted to create analogies between the play of form and emptiness and the alternation of yin and yang in the Taoist system, Jung's "enantiodromic interchange of opposites." This cannot be a sound analogy, because in the Buddhist view both yin and yang are form: they both emerge from emptiness. Emptiness in Taoism is characterized as "The Great Void," but in Buddhism emptiness is a quality of form, not an entity in itself.
6. Karmic vision: the habitual ways in which we view events and circumstances and how we respond to them.
7. Ngakpa Chögyam, *op.cit.*, p. 188.

Chapter Two: Approaching the Tiger

1. Ngakpa Chögyam, *Wearing the Body of Visions* (Ramsey, NJ: Aro Books, 1995), p. 180.
2. Chagdüd Tulku, *Lord of the Dance* (Junction City, CA: Padma Publishing, 1992), pp. 113–114.
3. Patrul Rinpoche, *The Words of My Perfect Teacher* (*Kunzang Lama'i Shelung*) (New York: Harper Collins, 1994), pp. 138–139. A collection of stories about Do-khyentsé and Dza Paltrül is being compiled by Ngak'chang Rinpoche for Aro Books.
4. "Repugnance for samsara" means the sense of having exhausted indulgence in one's own coping strategies in life to the extent that not only the result they bring, but even these self-defeating processes themselves, have become burdensome, aggravating, and no longer pleasurable. One has become unable to escape a nagging sense of suspicion that the basis of one's rationale might in fact be empty.
5. Jamgön Kongtrül, "Explanation of the Characteristics of the Master and Student Relationship, How to Follow the Master, and How to Teach and Listen to the Dharma" in *The Treasury of Knowledge* (*Shes-bya kun-khyab*), Vol. II, published as *The Teacher-Student Relationship*, tr. Ron Geary (Ithaca, NY: Snow Lion Publications, 1999).
6. Ngakpa Rig'dzin Shikpo (writing as Michael Hookham), *The Middle Way*, August, 1987.

7. Asvaghosa, *Fifty Verses of Guru Devotion* (Tib. *La-ma nga-chu-pa*, Skt. *Gurupañcasika*), tr. Translation Bureau of the Library of Tibetan Works and Archives (Library of Tibetan Works and Archives, 1975).
8. Asvaghosa, *op. cit.*
9. The retreat center of Lama Tharchin Rinpoche in the Santa Cruz Mountains of California.
10. Ngak'chang Rinpoche gave these teachings and empowerments in the autumn of 1999.
11. It is not necessary to take thirteen years to enter into vajra commitment. Thirteen years is considered the maximum time, which is to say that if one cannot establish vajra commitment in thirteen years, then it is necessary to seek another lama with whom one can establish it.
12. Ngakpa Chögyam, *op. cit.*, p. 176.

CHAPTER THREE: THE HEART OF VAJRAYANA

1. Dza Patrul Rinpoche, *The Words of My Perfect Teacher* (*Kun zang Lama'i Shelung*) (New York: Harper Collins, 1994), p. 145.
2. Keith Dowman, *Masters of Enchantment: The Lives and Legends of the Mahasiddhas* (Rochester, VT: Inner Traditions International, 1988), p. 111.
3. Tulku Thondup, *Hidden Teachings of Tibet: An Explanation of the Terma Tradition of Tibetan Buddhism*, ed. By Harold Talbot (Ithaca, NY: Snow Lion Publications, 1997).
4. Third Dodrup Chen Rinpoche, *"Wonder Ocean: An Explanation of the Dharma Treasure Tradition"* (*gTer Gyi rNam Shad*) in Tulku Thondüp, *Hidden Teachings of Tibet* (Boston: Wisdom Publications, 1986), p. 157. gTértöns are discoverers of hidden dharma treasures.
5. From an unpublished letter to the author.
6. Padmasambhava, *Dakini Teachings: Padmasambhava's Oral Instructions to Lady Tsogyal*, tr. Eric Pema Kunsang (Boston: Shambhala Publications, 1990), pp. 103–104.
7. Dilgo Khyentsé, *The Wish Fulfilling Jewel* (Boston: Shambhala Publications, 1988), pp. 3–4.
8. Asvaghosa, *Fifty Verses of Guru Devotion* (Tib. *La-ma nga-chu-pa*, Skt. *Gurupañcasika*), tr. Translation Bureau of the Library of Tibetan Works and Archives (Library of Tibetan Works and Archives, 1975).
9. Kalu Rinpoche, *The Foundations of Tibetan Buddhism* (previously published as *The Gem Ornament of Manifold Oral Instructions Which Benefits Each and Everyone Accordingly*) (Ithaca, NY: Snow Lion Publications, 1999), p. 119.
10. Asvaghosa, *op. cit.*

11. Understanding the lower realms as psychological states was not common in Tibet.
12. "On Receiving Initiation into the Vajrayana Path" included in *Advice to Those Receiving Wangs* (first pub. Jetsun Sakya Meditation Centre, reprinted by Ögyen Chöling [now the Rigpa Fellowship] for the visit of HH Sakya Trizin, 1977–78).
13. Chögyam Trungpa, *Journey Without Goal* (Boston: Shambhala Publications, 1985), p. 96.
14. Small sacred images, pressed from a mould into clay or dough, and empowered with the blessing of a lama.
15. Dza Patrul Rinpoche, *op. cit.*, pp. 143–153.
16. Tsele Natsok Rangdrol, *Empowerment and the Path of Liberation* (Leggett, CA: Rangjung Yeshe Publications, 1993), pp. 36–37.
17. Chögyam Trungpa, *Journey Without Goal* (Boston: Shambhala Publications, 1985), pp. 96–97.

CHAPTER FOUR: A TIME OF TRANSITION

1. In Buddhism, concept consciousness is regarded as one of the senses in addition to sight, hearing, touch, taste and smell.
2. The notably outrageous mahasiddha Drukpa Künlegs once scoffed: "These intellectuals! When they're not talking about it they're writing about it. When they're not writing about it they're thinking about it."
3. Chögyam Trungpa, *Journey Without Goal* (Boston: Shambhala Publications, 2000), p. 50.
4. Chögyam Trungpa, *op. cit.*, pp. 88–89.
5. Chögyam Trungpa, *Crazy Wisdom* (Shambhala Publications, 1991), p. 64.

CHAPTER FIVE: THE ULTIMATE ADVENTURE

1. The term "western lama" applies to lamas who are western by birth rather than western in the sense of wishing to adapt Buddhism on the basis of psychotherapy and western political and philosophical ideas.
2. From the *Sixth Vajra Letter*, a privately distributed communication to personal students (quoted with permission).
3. Refuge is the formal act of expressing one's confidence in and commitment to the Buddhist path in general.
4. Karl Kraus, *Die Fackel*, 376/77, May 30, 1913, p. 21.
5. The Confederate Sanghas of Aro comprises the sanghas of the lineage holders of the Aro gTér and those of their disciples who are lineage lamas. So, Confederate Sanghas of Aro refers to the totality of the incarnate lineage.

6. The Aro gTér lineage has two kinds of ordination: ngakma/ngakpa and naljorma/naljorpa. These have differences as to style and path of practice, and wear different robes.
7. *Vision* 12/13, Summer 1998/Spring 1999 issue.

CHAPTER SIX: COMMON QUESTIONS ABOUT VAJRAYANA

1. *Sem-de*: "the series of the nature of Mind," the first of the three series of the Dzogchen *trek-chod*, in which direct introduction to one's own nature becomes possible.
2. Interview with Khenpo Sonam Tobgyal Rinpoche for the Aro sangha's online magazine, *Vision*, 2001.2. Hungry ghost (Skt. *preta*), those who can never be satisfied, no matter how much they consume.
3. Hungry ghost (Skt. *preta*), those who can never be satisfied, no matter how much they consume.